BREAKING
THROUGH THE LINES
THE MARION MOTLEY STORY

By David Lee Morgan Jr.

Mendota Heights, Minnesota

First Edition
First Printing, 2023

Cover and book design by Karli Kruse
Edited by Chrös McDougall

Photographs ©: Harry Hall/AP Images, cover; Pro Football Hall of Fame, 10, 26; Margaret Bowles/AP Images, 43; Jacob Boomsma/Shutterstock Images, 50; AP Images, 74, 95, 101, 124; Pro Football Hall of Fame/AP Images, 77, 89, 108, 112, 163; Harold Valentine/AP Images, 91, 103; Vernon J. Biever/AP Images, 130; Warren Bond Photography, 156; David Lee Morgan Jr., 167; PBS Western Reserve, 171; Matthew Cowles & Omega Jaricha, back cover

Press Box Books, an imprint of Press Room Editions.

ISBN
978-1-63494-753-4 (paperback)
978-1-63494-754-1 (ebook)

Library of Congress Control Number: 2023904675

Distributed by North Star Editions, Inc.
2297 Waters Drive,
Mendota Heights, MN 55120
www.northstareditions.com

Printed in Canada

To the greatest parents a sports-loving kid could ever have. Thank you, David Lee "Sonny" Morgan Sr. and Gwenn "The High-Note-Girl" Morgan. Everything I learned about loving life and reaching my potential, I learned from the both of you.

To my wife, Jill, my partner, my best friend, and a woman with the kindest heart in the world.

To my older sister, Terri, thanks for introducing me to the band that would become my favorite of all time, Steely Dan (Donald and Walter).

To my older brother, Devon, thanks for introducing me to karate, Bruce Lee, and Enter the Dragon *in the '70s.*

To my youngest sister, Dana, a classical pianist, thanks for being the most talented out of all of us.

To my cousin, "Mr. Intelligent" Richard Morgan. You taught me class, elegance, and style, and taught me to love family, beyond everything, because family is what matters most.

And to one of the biggest Cleveland Browns fans I know, my Aunt Posume, the "Homewood Avenue Browns Block Party Queen," and the ruler of the "Morgan Travel Club."

Love you all. This book is for you.

CONTENTS

FOREWORD BY PAUL WARFIELD

I grew up in a small, Northeast Ohio industrial town called Warren, where the steel industry was heavy and booming. As a youngster growing up in the mid to late 1940s after World War II, I was a tremendous follower of my hometown team, the Cleveland Browns, and certainly of Marion Motley. He was a focal point for me because he was one of the best players, not only on the Cleveland Browns, but in the entire National Football League. Mr. Motley was a trailblazer, as were Bill Willis, Kenny Washington, and Woody Strode, who all entered professional football when the number of African American players was minuscule, at best.

Ideally, one looks for individuals who have characteristics of that individual, and although I was a youngster and didn't understand all the complexities of what was going on in our society at the time, I certainly identified with Marion Motley because he was African American. I was a grammar-school kid at that point; however, I could certainly discern there were some differences in our society. The school system I went to in Warren was integrated, and the sports programs in which I participated in grammar school, junior high school and high school were fully integrated.

I knew of Marion Motley and his presence because he grew up nearby in Canton, about 50 miles from my hometown, and played for the high school (Canton McKinley Senior High School) that I would play against as a youngster when I started my high school scholastic football career at Warren G. Harding High School. I am in awe of those who came before me, and particularly Motley, because of his roots in Ohio and the proximity of his hometown of Canton to mine.

When I joined the Browns organization right out of college in 1964, Marion Motley was still an integral part of the Cleveland Browns legacy, as were fellow African American players Willis; Horace Gillom, who played at the high school level for Paul Brown at Massillon High School; and Lenny Ford.

Motley lived in Cleveland, and I personally got to know him and became a friend of his. He was a very personable individual. Our relationship grew because Motley still loved the Cleveland Browns' organization after he retired, and occasionally he would come to our practice sessions when I was with the team. My personal relationship stemmed from there. Later on, once I picked up the game of golf, we would play an occasional round at a local club in Cleveland where he enjoyed playing.

A side of him that I gained an appreciation for is that everyone remembered him as this tough, rugged guy on the field, but his personality was very mild and father-like. He was a part of the Cleveland Browns alumni, remained part of the Browns tradition, and gave me all of the encouragement possible because he wanted me to succeed as a Cleveland Brown.

As I said, I joined the National Football League in 1964, and it was a very specialized era when players no longer played both ways. However, Motley was a two-way player: a prolific fullback with tremendous speed and rugged power, but additionally, he played defense and was an outstanding linebacker.

Motley was the last of the great two-way football players. More than that, he was a great man.

— Paul Warfield, Pro Football Hall of Fame, Class of 1983

Over his 13-year NFL career as a wide receiver with the Cleveland Browns (1964–69, 1976–77) and Miami Dolphins (1970–74), Paul Warfield was an eight-time Pro Bowl selection and First-Team All-Pro selection in 1971 and 1973. He was also a two-time Super Bowl champion with the Dolphins, the first as a member of the team's undefeated 1972 season. Prior to his pro career, Warfield was an all-state football player and track star at Warren G. Harding High School in Warren, Ohio, and later was an All-Big Ten football player and two-time letterwinner in track at The Ohio State University.

Marion Motley helped reintegrate pro football in 1946, then went on to become one of the dominant players of his era.

INTRODUCTION:

WHO WAS MARION MOTLEY?

Blood trickled from his muscular Black hands as white football players dug their cleats into them.

Teeth were knocked out of his mouth.

His life was threatened on many occasions.

They did not want Negroes on the field.

The year was 1946. Jim Crow laws, segregation, and racial discrimination against Black people were openly and lawfully enforced. Yet in the face of this racism, four Black football players changed the American sports landscape forever. A year before Jackie Robinson famously broke the "color line" in Major League Baseball, Marion Motley, Woody Strode, Kenny Washington, and Bill Willis reintegrated American professional sports. Motley and Willis signed with the Cleveland Browns in the newly formed All-America Football Conference. They followed Strode and Washington, who had signed with the National Football League's Los Angeles Rams a few months earlier.

Strode and Washington, who were older and past their primes, struggled in Los Angeles and didn't last long in the league. Willis, a defensive lineman, went on to have a Hall of Fame career.

Still, Motley's career by far was the best of the four. A thunderous fullback standing 6'1" and weighing 232 pounds, Motley played nine pro seasons from 1946–55, eight with the Browns and his last season with the Pittsburgh Steelers. A constant threat to bulldoze through defensive lines, Motley twice led his league in rushing yards and for his career averaged 5.7 yards per carry. For much of his career, when the opposing team took possession, Motley transitioned into a feared linebacker. He also returned 48 kicks over the years, averaging more than 23 yards per return. Motley's prowess helped make the Browns the dominant team in the AAFC, a status that carried into the NFL when they joined that league in 1950.

"I was as big as the linemen I ran against, so I didn't worry about them," Motley said in a quote shared on the Pro Football Hall of Fame website. "And once I ran over a back twice, I didn't have to run over him a third time. He had reservations by then."

Motley's accomplishments on the gridiron never reached the national consciousness like those of Robinson, whose sport was much more popular than pro football at the time. But in his hometown of Canton, Ohio, which is only an hour south of Cleveland, Motley remained a revered figure into his retirement. Never was that adoration greater than in 1968, when he was inducted into the Pro Football Hall of Fame in Canton. He became only its second Black member.

As time passed, though, Motley's status dimmed even in Canton. It was in that context that PBS Western Reserve produced a half-hour, Regional Emmy Award–winning documentary, *Lines Broken: The Story of Marion Motley*, that helped reignite interest in the former star (editor's note: and for which the author of this book served as a co-producer). In an interview for that film, which premiered in February 2021, longtime *USA Today* NFL columnist Jarrett Bell pointed out that Motley "played in an era where players routinely played both ways, and he was probably the most dominating big back in NFL history."

Bell compared Motley to two other Hall of Fame backs in Bronko Nagurski and Jerome Bettis. "And Motley was probably better than both of those guys," Bell said. "The statistics will tell you that. He averaged almost six yards a carry, which is the most ever still for any fullback or running back. He was a great pass blocker in a time when the passing game really started to get some legs, if you will. But he was also a great linebacker, so if Motley had never played fullback, he would have been an all-class linebacker, and that's what we would be talking about."

Bell went on to say: "If you think about the cartoon character of the big bruising guy who was twice as big as the people trying to tackle him and he's just bowling over them, and guys bouncing off of him when he got into the open field, that was Motley. He truly was a man against boys in a lot of situations."

Antonio Hall played at some of the highest levels of the sport, starring as an offensive lineman at the University of Kentucky before moving on to a pro career in Canada. Before that, he played for some of the most storied high school teams in Ohio history at Canton McKinley High School. His Bulldogs teams won back-to-back state titles in 1997 and 1998, and a *USA Today* mythical national championship in the first of those years. Two of his teammates, safety Mike Doss and defensive lineman Kenny Peterson, went on to Ohio State and then the NFL. The Bulldogs' quarterback, Josh McDaniels, developed into one of the NFL's most esteemed offensive coordinators with the New England Patriots, and in 2022 became head coach of the Las Vegas Raiders. The Canton McKinley head coach during that era was Thom McDaniels, Josh's dad. One of the legendary high school football coaches in Ohio history, Thom led the Bulldogs from 1982 to 1997 and again in 2014.

Hall, who graduated from Canton McKinley in 2000, returned two decades later to become the school's head football coach and athletic director. A half-century removed from Motley's time on the field, Hall found that most students there had no idea about the school's most famous alum.

"Time has a way of washing away a legacy," Hall said. "Over the years, I have asked over 500 of my history students if they could identify Marion Motley, and not one of them could say who he was or what he had accomplished. Young African Americans of today must know that the hardships Motley endured all those years ago made the opportunities they have today possible. Citizens of Canton and Stark County must acknowledge that one of our favorite sons made the world a better place through social justice, and students of Canton McKinley must realize that if a fellow graduate can change the world, so can you. Canton made. Bulldog proud. As we like to say, you can get there from here."

The students at Canton McKinley aren't the only ones whose awareness of the sport's Black pioneers is incomplete. Bell recalled the passing of Willis in 2007. At the time, Bell was covering the Baltimore Ravens.

"I went into the Ravens' locker room," Bell said, "and I started asking players, 'Do you know who Bill Willis was?' Not a soul knew." Bell recalled Ray Lewis, the Ravens' star linebacker at the time, along with safety Ed Reed and offensive tackle Jonathan Ogden were interested in knowing more about Willis. Notably, all three are now in the Hall of Fame themselves.

"They were saying, 'Tell us more,' and I remember Ray's reaction," Bell said. "I was like, 'You know, Ray, (Willis) was like the first middle linebacker. He played middle guard and the transition . . . That's the position that became your position, middle linebacker.' I mean, these guys were very respectful. They wanted to hear more and more."

Whether you are a sports fan or not, Motley's life and his accomplishments on and off the football field are important parts of American history. His story needs to be told and never forgotten. What he stood for should be celebrated in Canton, throughout the state of Ohio, and across the country.

CHAPTER I

1968: A YEAR THAT CHANGED AMERICA

The 1960s were a turbulent time in the United States, with racial and social unrest and civil rights awareness at the forefront. Dr. Martin Luther King Jr. was assassinated in April 1968. That June, Robert Kennedy, a leading candidate for the Democratic nomination for president and a prominent civil rights supporter—not to mention the brother of former president John F. Kennedy—also was assassinated. Riots and violence spread throughout cities across the country. At the same time, the United States was engaged in an unpopular war in Vietnam.

Yet, on the sports landscape, 1968 was a breakout year for Black athletes. That May, Bill Russell became the first Black head coach to win a major American professional sports championship when he did so as a player-coach for the Boston Celtics. Four months later Arthur Ashe became the first Black man to win a major tennis title when he won the U.S. Open. And 1968 was also the year when Marion Motley received the announcement he had hoped to hear.

On February 19, 1968, the Pro Football Hall of Fame

announced Motley was one of seven inductees to that year's class, joining Cliff Battles, Art Donovan, Elroy "Crazy Legs" Hirsch, Wayne Millner, Charley Trippi, and Alex Wojciechowicz. It was the perfect culmination of a historic career that changed professional sports forever.

Prior to Motley, the Hall had inducted just one Black player, defensive back Emlen Tunnell, in 1967. Tunnell was the first Black player to sign and play for the New York Giants, in 1948, and after ending his career with the Green Bay Packers, he retired in 1961 as the holder of NFL records for interceptions (79), interception return yards (1,282), punt returns (258), and punt return yards (2,209).

Though Tunnell beat Motley by a year, Motley's selection hit differently, at least around Canton. Tunnell had played 14 seasons, with all but the last three in New York. "But nobody knew him, at least not in Canton," recalled Stephen Perry, the former Pro Football Hall of Fame president and executive director. "Maybe some people that were football aficionados knew him. (Former Hall of Fame Executive Director) Joe Horrigan probably knew everything about Emlen Tunnell; most people didn't know anything about him."

Perry, a Canton native who is also Black, continued: "But when Marion Motley went in, that was different. He was a hometown guy, and that was a big thing. I'd like to be able to say that everyone was thrilled and happy that, at the time, the second Black man was being inducted into the Pro Football Hall of Fame. I'm sure there was some resentment, and that some people didn't think that was the right thing, but, as it related to the Black community, there was a lot of pride."

That pride felt around Canton extended to the Black communities around the country during a year of unrest for many Black Americans.

"Sports enabled people to bond and work together and just focus on their ability to get the job done and not care about economic status or race or ethnicity or anything else," Perry said. "That's why I think in '68, you had two different worlds. You had the world where some entertainers and some sports figures were being lauded for what they were accomplishing, but the rest of the professions were not receiving that same kind of thing."

Charita M. Goshay is a Canton native who has worked at the *Canton Repository* newspaper since 1990, eventually becoming a nationally syndicated columnist for GateHouse Media. Goshay, who is Black, has always had her finger on the pulse of what was going on in the area, and especially the critical issues that resonated within the Black community. Motley's induction in 1968 was one of those moments.

"America has always been a country of dualities," said Goshay, who is also a member of the *Repository*'s editorial board. "With the '60s, you had the race riots and Woodstock and all that, so America has always been a country of duality, culturally."

Goshay said she was about 12 years old in 1968 and remembered the turmoil of that time, especially from a Black perspective. "I was a geeky kid because I loved history, news, and politics," she said. "I can remember the night Martin Luther King was killed and being afraid . . . of what? I don't know. I just remember being afraid . . . maybe afraid for my country. But at the same time, I think (Black) people needed things like the Hall of Fame, ceremonies, inductions, parades, and celebration. I think we needed that.

"Football has always been, at least in the modern era, a place where people on margins can be part of the larger picture," continued Goshay, who prides herself on being a "lifelong suffering but faithful" Cleveland Browns fan. "It's a good thing that someone like Marion Motley is in the Hall of Fame. He is someone who obviously deserved it. There's no question about it."

Added Perry: "In the '60s, and the civil rights era, times were tense and there were difficult days for Blacks in this country, and in Canton, but the Black community was proud of Motley's induction. The NFL was recognizing the performance of a Black individual to the extent that they were inducting him to the highest honor that a football player could receive."

Perry continued: "I often have thought that sports and maybe the military are two of the institutions where people put color aside and put ethnic background aside and put economic status aside. If you're in a foxhole with a buddy, and your life depends on him, and his life depends on you, he doesn't care what color you are. It doesn't matter where your parents came from. He just cares that you do your job, and he does his job so that we all survive. Well, the same thing is true to a lesser extent in football. If you're the right tackle and I'm the right guard, I don't really care where your parents are from. I just care that you make your block and I make my block and we win. I think sports brings that out."

Motley's induction was the definitive affirmation that his merits on the field warranted nothing less than him joining the sport's all-time greats in the Hall of Fame, in his hometown of

Canton. And his close friend and fellow pioneering Browns team-mate, Bill Willis, was right by his side supporting Motley, like he always had.

"I am extremely proud and happy that the committee saw fit to induct Marion Motley into the Hall of Fame," Willis said during a banquet honoring Motley's forthcoming induction. "Actually, the Hall itself would become a farce if Motley was not inducted, because he is one of the truly great football players. There are always comparisons between Marion Motley and football players of today and yesterday, but really you just can't compare the guy because as an all-around football player, I don't think Motley had any peers."

Though the NFL had been around since 1920, and pro foot-ball about three decades longer, the Pro Football Hall of Fame inducted its first class only in 1963. Motley became the third Cleveland Brown to achieve the honor, joining quarterback Otto Graham (Class of '65) and coach Paul Brown (Class of '67). "I couldn't be prouder to be in a Hall of Fame with any other man," Brown said during the banquet in Motley's honor, held by the Intra-American Sports Club.

***

Cleveland Mayor Carl Stokes, the first Black mayor of a major U.S. city, proclaimed March 13, 1968, as "Marion Motley Day" in Cleveland. And on May 4, 1968, the city of Canton held its own "Marion Motley Day," a celebration that included a parade through downtown and a banquet at the Moonlight Ballroom at Meyers Lake Park. Community leaders presented Motley with a key to the city, a golden sheriff's deputy badge, and a proclamation. He also received a new car.

The day was also a lifetime event for Ruth Chenault, who served as Motley's escort during the parade and festivities. At the time, the Hall of Fame called upon the cheerleaders from Canton McKinley High School to escort the inductees, and Chenault, as a senior and the head cheerleader, got the honor of walking with Motley. In a 2019 interview, Chenault relived the day, recalling specific details like it was yesterday. "(The driver) picked me up and drove me to the downtown Motor Inn, which was where Marion and his wife were staying," she recalled. "They were eating breakfast in the dining room, and that's where I met them."

After breakfast, Chenault said they all got in the car, a beautiful red convertible sedan, and rode to the popular Mayfair Tavern downtown, which was close to their spot in the parade lineup. Chenault said she even got the chance to meet actor Pat O'Brien, who played the lead role in the film *Knute Rockne All American*. "That was a thrill meeting a big star like that," Chenault said. "I'd been watching his movies all my life."

As the parade started, Chenault recalled that Motley and Willis were in the back of the car. Willis was in the seat, but Motley was sitting atop the back portion of the car so that he could wave to the crowd as the parade progressed. She said there was only one drawback to the parade. "We got in the car and, unfortunately, in the lineup for some strange reason, they put us right ahead of the Tigers' swing band."

The band was that of Canton McKinley's fiercest rival, the Massillon Washington Tigers, and the band's signature song was, and still is, "Tiger Rag." "We went through the entire parade route listening to 'Tiger Rag,' and if you listen to that song for as many hours as we did, the song wears on you," Chenault said.

"Even if it was a beautiful song that I loved, it would've bothered me and wore on me because it was played by our number one enemy." Still, the entire day was such a thrill for Chenault, and the teenager was basking in it all. "I was in the front seat, and my face hurt from smiling hour after hour because that's a pretty slow drive they take," she said.

Later that day, the Dallas Cowboys and Chicago Bears met in the Hall of Fame Game at Fawcett Stadium, which was later renovated and is now called Tom Benson Hall of Fame Stadium. At halftime, the convertible drove onto the field and the occupants got out. A friendly man noticed Chenault getting autographs and offered some advice that she still remembers. "He told me to make sure I also get Bill Willis's autograph, because he would be in the Hall of Fame soon," Chenault said. "I did follow his advice, and he was right. Years later, Bill Willis went into the Hall of Fame." Willis was inducted in 1977.

As for the halftime ceremony, Motley received a tremendous reception from his hometown fans. "It was a massive, loud crowd," Chenault recalled. "He was the hometown hero, there was no doubt about that. And to be truthful, I was actually hamming it up because that's kind of my nature. I walked my walk and held (Motley's) hand as I walked out smiling in case anybody was taking pictures, which of course I knew they were, because I could see the photographers lined up. It was my moment to shine. I knew they were not there to see me, but I was not going to make him ashamed of me."

Chenault didn't have to worry about that because she was wearing a new cheerleading uniform. Was it ordered from a catalog? By no means. It was custom made by a gentleman in

Canton. "That man happened to be my cousin, and at that time, he was known around here as the Godfather of Fashion," Chenault said. "The whole day was just wonderful."

Years passed since that momentous occasion for Chenault. She said it's important that children today remember Motley's legacy. "I've spent so much time with children (over the years), and I know there's a generation that really doesn't know his contributions."

***

The banquet ahead of Motley's induction included a who's-who of pro football dignitaries, including former Cleveland Browns coach Paul Brown and some of Motley's Browns teammates, including Willis, Otto Graham, Lou Groza, and Dante Lavelli. An estimated 600 people came out to celebrate. "I just can't get over the size of this gathering and the way you feel about this man," said Brown, Cleveland's groundbreaking head coach from 1946 to 1962. Motley was equally impressed. "I am overwhelmed with the turnout today. There are no words to try to express the feeling," Motley said, trying to gather his thoughts while taking in the adulation. "This car and the people turning out was just a tremendous thing. It's a great day for me."

Twenty-two years earlier, when Motley broke through the color line with the Browns, he did so alongside Willis. The pair battled together on the field at a time when many whites didn't want them there, and Willis remained right by Motley's side at the ceremony. "Motley, I'm so proud for you," Willis said. "I think this is wonderful, being able to come back to your own hometown and being received like this. You've been out of the city of Canton for quite some time, and to come back to all of this, this in itself is splendid. There's nothing like going back home."

The football world knew all about Motley's offensive exploits, Willis said, but most people didn't know Motley was also a fantastic middle linebacker. When playing together on the defensive side of the ball, Willis recalled, the two flexed their competitive muscles in a game to see who could record the most tackles. "But Motley played really close behind me, so he had the habit of taunting the opponents," Willis recalled. "He did this to (New York Giants running back) Buddy Young, and of course Buddy would always take up the challenge. And every time Buddy Young would come through that hole, he would make two or three yards and ol' Motley would tackle him. Motley would taunt him again. 'OK Mr. Five-by-Five, come right down here.' Again, Buddy Young would come through that hole, and he would make four or five yards, and so I got just a little discouraged. I looked up at Motley and said, 'Now wait a minute. Now, it's all right for you to taunt Buddy Young. But every time you make those tackles, he's running over me in order for you to get to him.'"

Young played professional football for nine years, going against Motley in both the AAFC and the NFL. In 1964, Young became the first Black executive hired by a major sports league when the NFL did so. Four years later, he too attended the banquet to honor Motley.

In his remarks, Young spoke of being grateful for the opportunities afforded to him through sports. Football allowed him to be recognized for his abilities on the field—his wins and losses, and his professional success off the field as an NFL executive—instead of being judged by his race. "Marion Motley exemplified this 20 years ago," Young said. To Motley, Young said, it wasn't about who his teammates were, but that they were his teammates. "He did his job because that's what it was all about," Young said.

Graham, for his part, said he never judged Motley by his skin color. "Color doesn't mean a thing," the Browns' record-setting quarterback said. "It's what kind of man are you? What do you have down deep inside your heart, and what kind of a job do you do? It's as simple as that." Graham then looked at Motley's mother and said, "Mrs. Motley, other people have said this, but you should be very, very proud. I add my congratulations to you because you have raised one of the nicest guys, a great football player, but most important, one of the nicest guys, one of the best men, a man's man, and this is the important thing."

The sentiment was shared by Brown and others. Motley was revered for the type of person he was throughout his career, and even after his playing days were over, beloved both for the man he was and the way he played the game.

"I will say to you that if it could all be just like it was in football, where you're just a person and you play if you're good enough—it's the man-to-man proposition—we could certainly have a lot happier existence," Brown said.

Meanwhile, teammate and Hall of Famer Lavelli shared a funny story about Motley falling asleep as Brown was addressing the team. "We're playing a rival team, the Giants or something, and Paul Brown is up in front of the class, talking to us, telling us about the Sunday game," Lavelli said. "Marion was sitting in the back of the room sleeping. Paul Brown always had a towel up there he used to erase the blackboard with. He grabbed a hold of this towel and popped Marion right in the face. It sure woke Marion up in a hurry."

***

When Motley was inducted into the Hall of Fame on August 3, 1968, Willis was his presenter. "Whenever you think of the Cleveland Browns, you must think of Paul Brown—really," Willis said, in part. "Whenever you think of Paul Brown, you think of Marion, and you think of Otto Graham. But you can neither think of Otto Graham, the Paul Browns, or the Cleveland Browns without thinking of Marion Motley. He was truly a complete football player."

Marion Motley, shown at his 1968 induction ceremony, became only the second Black member of the Pro Football Hall of Fame.

Motley's Hall of Fame speech was one of the shortest in Hall of Fame history. His humility may have been the reason.

Thank you, Bill, and I'd like to thank the many friends that have come to pay tribute to seven of us today. I look out over this crowd, and I see many faces that I know that I've gone to school with. And it makes a person being from his hometown, of being presented into the Hall of Fame, in the hometown. It's a wonderful feeling. I've been asked many times in the last two or three days as to how you feel, or what will be your feeling. Well, trying to express or say how you feel about this, going into the Hall of Fame, it's rather hard. I'd like to thank the many teammates that I've played with that helped me to be the so-called player that I was at that particular time. Fellows like Bill Willis, Lin Houston, Cliff Lewis, Dante Lavelli, and many others that I could go on and name, but it would take quite a while. But I'd just like to say again, I'd like to thank everyone for coming and thank the people that inducted me into the Hall of Fame. Thank you very much.

CHAPTER 2

THE GREAT NORTHERN MIGRATION TO CANTON

Cross burnings.

Lynchings.

The Ku Klux Klan in white-hooded sheets terrorizing and committing violent acts against Blacks.

These were regular occurrences seen and experienced by Black people living in the South during the early 1920s, including the Motleys of Leesburg, Georgia, a small town in the southwest part of the state. Overt racism was rampant in rural Southern communities like Leesburg, while discriminatory Jim Crow laws established in the late 1870s enforced racial segregation in an effort to prevent any economic, political, or social gains for Black people. According to the Martin Luther King Jr. National Historical Park in Atlanta, the Jim Crow laws in effect during the 1920s in Georgia barred everything from interracial marriage to Black barbers cutting the hair of white women to whites selling wine or beer to Blacks, and vice versa. And that's to say nothing of the enforced segregation in restaurants, parks, and sports.

It was within this context that the Motleys and many other Black families decided to pack their belongings, regardless of how little they had, and leave. Millions of Blacks left the South in an exodus that stretched from 1916–70 and is now known as the Great Migration. They moved to cities in the North, Midwest, and West for a new way a life. Northeastern Ohio, home to cities like Canton and nearby Akron, was a popular destination owing to the local industry offering abundant jobs.

"In the Canton area, there was the Hoover Company (vacuums), Timken Steel, Republic Steel, and there was Hercules Motor Manufacturing getting ready for the Second World War in the 1930s," Stark County historian Richard Haldi said. "Hercules was the largest manufacturer of engines for the government. So that was a huge draw for people from the South."

In 1920, Canton was also still in the glow of its contribution to the country. William McKinley had been born in 1843 in Niles, Ohio, but moved 50 miles southwest to Canton at age nine. He later returned to the city, after serving in the Ohio Volunteer Infantry during the American Civil War, to set up a law practice. In 1896, he was elected the 25th president of the United States.

McKinley's rise brought a lot of attention to Canton, which wasn't a large town. Though his legacy will always be defined most by his assassination in 1901, McKinley's impact on Canton was tangible. In 1900, there were about 30,000 people in the city. By 1920, when the Motley family arrived, the population had swelled to around 85,000.

"Think about what a change that must've been for the 700 or so (Black) people from the little town of Leesburg, Georgia, way south, and I mean they were deep in the South," Haldi said. "And then up in Canton, the population was about 7,000 Black people alone. Coming from rural Georgia, it had to be a big adjustment for the Motleys."

The Motleys' move was spurred in part by a specific opportunity. A businessman for whom Marion's grandmother worked in Georgia had bought a company in Canton that forged steel, a process that involved heating the steel at high temperatures so it could be molded into shapes. In search of workers, the businessman traveled back to Georgia to find anyone interested in moving to Canton. Marion's father, Shakeful (the Professional Football Researchers Association has his name as Shakvol), and his mother, Blanche, decided to take their young son and start a new life in Ohio. According to Haldi, however, it wasn't much better for the Motleys and other Blacks who moved from the Deep South to Canton.

"The Klan involvement in Canton was strong at the time the Motleys arrived in 1920," Haldi said. In fact, the Klan had long held a presence in the area, dating to the McKinley era. One hotbed was in Minerva, about 17 miles southeast of Canton, Haldi said, while small communities such as Louisville to the north also harbored Klan members. In Canton, it wasn't uncommon for the Klan to hold marches down Market Avenue to the fairgrounds. The rise of prohibition in 1920, when the U.S. government banned the manufacture, sale, and transportation of alcoholic beverages, only made things worse. "Because their selling tactic, or whatever you want to call it, was Christianity and no booze," Haldi said. "That was the righteous push." The result, Haldi said, was a city that was less welcoming to Blacks than those moving to Canton had hoped. "When the

Motleys arrived, they didn't get away from the KKK by coming up from South Georgia," Haldi said.

Marion was three when his family moved to Canton. The wealthier population lived in the northeast and northwest parts of Canton. Families with modest means lived on the western side of the city, and these families typically owned their homes. The Motleys lived in the eastern part of the city in tenement housing, low-income housing units for families all living and working closely together. Most of the Black population at that time rented—and struggled to make rent.

Conditions were poor, and because of that, criminal activity such as bootlegging was common. This illegal liquor trafficking was in response to prohibition, which remained in effect until 1933.

"Whiskey runs" were frequent in Canton, and the liquor was delivered secretly by car in five-gallon cans, many times in the cover of darkness. The police used to chase these whiskey runners with their deliveries through the Motleys' neighborhood. In fact, most of the criminal activity was in their neighborhood. The high crime rate was because most of the residents were poor and could not do anything about it.

Though Jim Crow laws weren't in effect in Ohio, Blacks were effectively excluded from the city's wealthier northeast and northwest areas. And it wasn't just the Black families that were frowned upon in certain areas of the city—so were poor Greeks, Italians, and other struggling ethnic groups that moved to Canton for the same reason as the Motleys, looking for a better life.

Charita Goshay, the Canton native and longtime Black journalist for the *Canton Repository*, recalled that one branch of her family tree arrived in 1923 when her great-grandfather was recruited to install telephone poles. "There were only so many places that you could go to find work," she said. "It probably was word of mouth in a lot of cases, or you followed a family who were already here. That was the neighborhood where you had Italian and Greek immigrants, and Blacks, and they all pretty much got along pretty well."

The rough-and-tough area on the southeast side of town where the Motleys lived was referred to as "the Jungle." The Motley family first lived at 8th Street and Madison Avenue SE and later moved a couple of blocks to 10th Street and Lafayette Avenue SE. Black life in Canton was centered around a nearby section of Cherry Avenue SE, often referred to as Cherry Street. The neighborhood, which was almost entirely demolished during the 1970s to make way for a highway overpass, was an area where Blacks flourished even though they were discriminated against. According to Goshay, there were more than 100 businesses on those 13 blocks of Cherry Avenue, and 90 percent of them were Black owned.

"There was kind of an unspoken understanding that there were certain parts of town where you were apt to feel it would be more welcome than others," Goshay said. So those living in the vicinity of Cherry Avenue created their own oasis, their own world, out of necessity. "You had the business owners. The Black doctors had their offices there, along with the Black attorneys and Black store owners," she said. But Cherry Street was also where the gamblers and musicians and all the people in between gathered. Goshay described the eclectic mix of people as "the rogues and the role models" where everyone got along.

In Motley's neighborhood, the kids came from diverse backgrounds but were all poor, he recalled. But they were nonetheless close.

"Most of the neighborhood was Italian," Motley told the *Repository* in 1998. "We all played together, ran around together. If you were at someone's house and it was time to eat, they fed all the kids. It didn't matter if you were black or white."

Regardless of where they all came from—Blacks, Italians, Greeks—the families were all in the same situation. They were people living in poverty and being discriminated against because of their race, ethnicity, or both, and as such they weren't integrated within the larger white society. On and around Cherry Avenue, Italian- and Greek-owned grocery stores would let poor families like the Motleys set up a tab to buy groceries. There was camaraderie because they understood they all weren't necessarily welcomed, but they were going to survive and stick together because they all had something in common.

***

Though Shakeful and Blanche Motley didn't follow sports, the family happened to move to the birthplace of modern professional football. Marion was born on June 5, 1920, the same year the American Professional Football Association was founded in Canton. The local team, the Canton Bulldogs, was an early power, and after the league changed its name to the National Football League in 1922, the Bulldogs won the first two NFL championships, that year and in 1923. Decades later, Canton citizens pushed for the league to make its city home of the Pro Football Hall of Fame, and that happened when the building opened to the public on September 7, 1963.

During the 1920s, however, Black people were excluded from almost everything in American society, including sports. That didn't stop young Marion from taking a keen interest.

The Motleys' tenement housing was next to a playground. As older boys played football in an adjacent field, young Marion watched how they would get down in a crouched position facing the other side, then spring to their feet to block and tackle one another. Watching the older boys, Marion could have had no idea that one day he would be one of the greatest to ever play the sport.

One Sunday afternoon when Marion was about six or seven, his mother sent him on an errand to his cousin's house. His cousin didn't live too far away, and when Marion arrived, he heard someone inside listening to a football game on the radio.

Marion recalled the memory fondly. He loved listening to football games as a boy, and on this day the experience left him particularly inspired.

When it was time for him to walk home, Marion got down on his hands and knees in a football-like stance, imitating the older boys in the park, and acted as if he were playing in a football game. He ran around, making moves and cuts like he was running the football to avoid being tackled, before falling to the ground like he was tackled after a long run.

He did this not knowing his mother was watching from their kitchen window. That was OK, though, because she didn't know, or understand, what her son was doing, or why the boy was running and darting back and forth, then throwing himself to the ground.

It happened to be raining on this day, so when Marion fell to the ground during his play, he was covered in mud. Once he got home and walked inside, his mother asked what he was doing. Marion replied innocently, "playing football."

That was the start of Marion Motley's historic football career.

CHAPTER 3

EARLY DAYS ON THE GRIDIRON

The football bug bit Marion Motley in the butt, and by his early teens he had his sights set on joining the team at Canton's Central Junior High School. However, he soon realized that the football journey he was about to embark on would be filled with challenges—ones he would face for most of his life.

The first came when he decided to play football but didn't have a uniform. He produced a uniform of his own.

And it was an honorable uniform.

"I had an uncle that was in World War I, and he had these khaki pants with the lace boots and the loops," Motley said years later as an adult. "I took those khaki pants and rolled them up and went out and tried out for the team."

This was a sport Marion knew he wanted to play. But, with Shakeful working long hours in the steel factory, he had no time to help his son learn more about the game. Blanche, meanwhile, was taking care of the home and didn't know anything about football. Nonetheless, Marion was driven to play, so he continued with tryouts. Not telling his parents he was trying out for the football team was one of the dilemmas facing the young teenager. And he did a pretty good job of hiding what he was up to. In fact, when he'd get home from practice, he would roll up his "uniform" and throw it under the front porch until the next day.

One day, his parents were driving past the field where he was trying out. Blanche took a quick glance at all the boys running and tackling on the field and thought she saw a big kid who looked like her son. Mothers have those instincts. They just know. Blanche said to her husband, "That looks like Marion down there in that group. I think I just saw Marion down on that field."

"Oh, no!" Shakeful responded. "That's not him. It can't be."

Mom, however, was right. It was Marion, and boy, did he have his parents fooled. He even admitted it years later. "Well, I can tell you one thing: I went on about four or five days before they really found out I had snuck those pants out and went to the football field," he said.

Approximately 35 kids were trying out for the team. Between drills one day, they stood around waiting for their turn to try to impress the coaches. As Marion waited for his chance to show off his talents, he thought about all those days running errands for his mom when he acted like he was playing football as he moved through the back alley. Marion was excited and nervous, but he was ready for his opportunity.

The coaches, seeing that Marion was bigger than most of the other boys, put him at offensive tackle. When the tryout was over, head coach Danny Myers knew what he needed to do: "Get him a uniform!" he ordered the coaching staff. "Get him a uniform and get him in here tomorrow!"

Marion was thrilled. He'd proven he belonged on that team, and now he couldn't wait to finally tell his parents. Meanwhile,

Marion's teammates were glad to have him on the team. They were also glad the team was going to issue him pads. He was bigger, stronger, and faster than every other player on the team, and he was putting a hurting on some of his teammates, even though he wasn't wearing pads and they were. So, in a way, Marion's pads were protection for his teammates, not for him.

CHAPTER 4

THE MAKING OF A HIGH SCHOOL LEGEND

Each August, before the NFL season starts in earnest, tens of thousands of fans flock back to Northeastern Ohio and make Canton the center of the pro football universe for a weekend. Before the next class is inducted into the Pro Football Hall of Fame, two NFL teams meet for a preseason game next door at Tom Benson Hall of Fame Stadium, named after the late owner of the New Orleans Saints. Today's game comes with all the glitz of the modern NFL, and most fans likely have no idea the history made there decades earlier, when a young Marion Motley shined for Canton McKinley High School on what was then Fawcett Stadium.

Motley's career at Fawcett Stadium began even before he stepped foot on the field. Construction began in 1937, when Motley would have been around 17 years old, and he actually helped build the venue, laying cement for the foundation on land that used to be a brickyard and a natural shale amphitheater.

By then, Motley had already established himself as an elite player for one of the state's perennial powerhouse teams. In that era, freshmen weren't allowed to play varsity sports, so it was his sophomore year in 1936–37 when he began his spectacular high school career as a three-sport athlete in basketball, football, and track. Though his prowess in football soon overshadowed the other sports, it didn't get off to the most promising of starts.

Motley, at 6'1" and 200 pounds, was one of the fastest and biggest players on the team. Playing him at running back was seemingly a no-brainer. Central Junior High coach Danny Myers had even given McKinley coach Johnny Reed a heads-up that he had a player coming in Motley who had the potential to be a star running back. Yet Reed had other ideas.

"Several years ago, Danny Myers told me about this young fellow at Central," Reed said years later at a banquet. "You're gonna have a good football player up there."

"Who's that?"

"Marion Motley."

"I'll tell you what we'll do with him. We'll start him in as a guard."

Motley followed the coach's orders and lined up at right guard, even though he knew Reed had him in the wrong position. "When I went to high school, there was about seven or eight of us Blacks on the team," Motley once said. "The only thing is, back in those days it was hard for Blacks to get anywhere. Originally, I was a lineman. In those days, they didn't want the Black students to get ahead of the white (students), so they put me on the line, although I was about the second fastest, well maybe the fastest (on the team.)"

Reed later explained his decision to play Motley on the offensive line instead of at running back, noting that the team already had a pretty good back. "For that whole year, his sophomore year, he spent as a guard, the running guard, he was a beautiful running guard," Reed said in a radio interview. "There's been arguments, pros and cons, as long as I can remember."

But one man who would later play a significant role in Motley's life, Paul Brown, did not buy Reed's reasoning. Before making his name in the pro ranks, Brown was the legendary head coach at Massillon Washington High School, the state's best team at the time and McKinley's bitter rival 10 miles to the west. Though not known to bad-mouth another coach, Brown made it clear at a reception years later that he didn't mind seeing McKinley's best player battling it out on the offensive line. "I was listening to Johnny Reed talk about having to leave Canton in a hurry, and the thought struck me that anybody that would play Motley at guard really should be put out in a hurry," Brown joked.

In Motley's junior year, he became one of the best running backs in the state, and it happened by fate—or stubbornness—depending on whom you ask. Motley showed up for preseason practices that year, but the starting fullback did not. Reed was in a tough situation. "We didn't have a fullback," Motley explained. Without one, the coach couldn't run plays in practice. "So then the coach told me, 'Motley, we're going to make you a back.'"

Emil Kamp was the back who failed to show up that day. "I got into it with one of the assistant coaches because (Reed) was (pushing) me too hard, and I quit the team," Kamp told the *Akron Beacon Journal* in October 1994. "By the time I agreed to come back, they already had a new guy working out at fullback. His name was Marion Motley."

Motley became the starting fullback, and Kamp was put on the offensive line. Motley took advantage of that opportunity, and in the first eight games he rushed for 950 yards and ten touchdowns on just 58 rushing attempts. That meant Motley averaged 16 yards every time he was handed the ball.

The last game of the season for McKinley was always against Massillon, and Motley appeared primed to have a great game against his rival. Instead, Reed decided to put Motley back on the offensive line in the biggest game of the year. And it was not Kamp, the kid who skipped practice at the beginning of the season, replacing Motley. It was another player, Harold "Tippy" Lockard, who had been injured for most of the season. Lockard later played at the University of Michigan, but he was not as good as Motley.

Putting Motley back on the line proved to be a costly decision as McKinley lost 19–6 in front of a crowd more than 14,000 fans. It was McKinley's only loss of the year, and Massillon's third straight win over its archrival.

The decision to put Motley in the trenches didn't last. By the start of his senior year in 1938, he was back at starting fullback. Meanwhile, Fawcett Stadium, though not yet completed, was ready to host games.

On September 17, 1938, in front of close to 10,000 fans, McKinley played its first game there. Only the north stands had been completed; temporary west stands were in place while fans overflowed onto a nearby hill. That was enough for Motley. Though playing primarily as a running back, Motley on one key play took a pitch and ran to the outside before stopping and launching a pass downfield. Motley's halfback pass to Nick Roman became the first touchdown pass in Fawcett Stadium history.

Motley also ran for four touchdowns and kicked three extra points as the Bulldogs defeated Canton Lehman High School 48–6.

Such highlights were plentiful during Motley's senior season. He finished with 1,228 yards on 69 attempts, which meant he averaged 17.8 yards every time he ran the ball. Though he was a running back, Motley was also a dangerous passer. That's because when he took a pitch outside, the entire defense had to converge to try to bring him down. Receivers became wide-open, and Motley at times would pull up and throw a perfect strike downfield. He threw for 454 yards and seven touchdowns as a senior.

Before it was Tom Benson Hall of Fame Stadium, home of the annual Hall of Fame Game, Fawcett Stadium was the playground for Marion Motley and the Canton McKinley Bulldogs.

Like the year before, McKinley and Massillon both went into their season-ending showdown undefeated. This time, Reed kept Motley in as his starting running back. The game was competitive, even after Massillon built a 12–0 lead into the third quarter. Late in the game, McKinley moved the ball deep into Massillon territory. With 10 yards to go, Motley got the handoff and took off toward the end zone. Massillon's Lin Houston (who later became Motley's teammate with the Browns) stopped him with a hard hit. Motley left the game on that play and never returned as Massillon held on to the 12–0 win.

Despite never beating Massillon in his high school career, Motley earned quite the compliment from Brown years later, before his induction into the Hall of Fame. "Canton McKinley's offense was built (around) him, and we spent a lot of time trying to just play one man," Brown said. "He was extremely big as a high school boy with tremendous speed then. . . . We did gang on Motley a bit. We had to if we were going to get out alive."

Motley went 25–3 during his high school career, with his only three losses coming against Massillon. After the 1938 season, several McKinley players were first- and second-team All-Ohio selections. But not Motley. He was third-team All-Ohio, and anyone who knew anything about football knew Motley should have been first-team All-Ohio. He was one of the best players in the state, perhaps even in the nation. To many, it was obvious why he was not a first-team all-state pick. Just as when his coach had lined him up in the trenches as a sophomore, it came down to his skin color.

Larry Phillips, an Ohio sports historian and author of *Ohio's Autumn Legends, Vol. 1*, said: "If they had a symbol of Mr. Football in Ohio, it should be carved out of Marion Motley's form. That is how spectacular he was. And it was one of the greatest schools in the state as far as competition level. He was a man among boys even then."

So why didn't Motley receive the awards and recognition he deserved after his high school career ended?

"It had to be racism," Phillips said. "That's the only thing that makes sense. He averaged over 17 yards per carry for his (high school) career—not just a year, for a career, which is incredible. He was clearly the best player on his team. He was clearly the best player in this region, which was the hotbed of Ohio high school football. The only thing that makes sense is racism."

CHAPTER 5

OFF TO COLLEGE, BUT WHERE?

"The big Negro."
"The colored giant."
"The Dusky Dynamiter."
"The big colored lad."

Y ou would think that a great high school running back like Marion Motley would have been recruited by major colleges across the country. Paul Brown sure did, describing Motley as an "elite national recruit." And yet he wasn't recruited. America still wasn't ready for Blacks to excel and have fair opportunities in society, even sports.

Although college football wasn't strictly segregated at the time, not many schools recruited Black players. Ohio State, just 130 miles away in Columbus, didn't recruit Motley. Neither did any other Big Ten school. In 2020, *Columbus Dispatch* sportswriter Bill Rabinowitz wrote an eye-opening article for the paper's Buckeye Xtra titled "Ohio State football's history with race a source of both shame and pride." It detailed how Frederick Patterson, who had a Black father and white mother, joined the team in 1891, the program's second season. Another Black player, Julius Tyler, followed five years later.

Yet it wasn't until 1929 that Ohio State had another Black player, Akron native William Bell. Then, in 1934, Francis Schmidt took over as head coach, and he never had one Black player on his team. The general feeling was that Schmidt, who was there through 1940, didn't recruit Motley, or any other Black players, because of their race. "Francis Schmidt should answer for that," Brown said later.

Brown took over for Schmidt as Ohio State head coach in 1941, and a year later he signed Bill Willis, a Black lineman from Columbus. Little did anyone know at the time how consequential that decision would be.

Meanwhile, a story in Massillon's *Evening Independent* newspaper reported that Motley had been offered a scholarship to play at what's now Clemson University in South Carolina. But when the school found out Motley was Black, the offer was pulled. If Motley didn't have a shot with northern schools in the Big Ten, there was no chance he was going to play for one of the top programs in the Deep South. The Southeastern Conference didn't have a Black varsity athlete in any sport until 1966, when Steve Martin joined the baseball team at Tulane University. Greg Page and Nate Northington at the University of Kentucky became the SEC's first Black football players soon after, though Page died before he could appear in a game.

Motley ended up going to South Carolina, but instead of Clemson he enrolled at South Carolina State College, a Historically Black College and University (HCBU) in Orangeburg. Fifteen years after Motley's family left the area because of the blatant racism towards Blacks, he returned for the same reason—seeking opportunity.

Soon after Motley arrived on campus, he knew it wasn't the right fit for him. Little is known about his time there—not even his stats from that 1939 season. What is known is that South Carolina wasn't the right fit, and Motley wanted out.

Word of Motley's situation got back to Jimmy Aiken. He had coached at Canton McKinley before Motley got there, then led the University of Akron for three seasons before accepting the head coaching job at the University of Nevada in Reno in 1939. Though Aiken hadn't coached Motley in high school, he knew of the player's ability. When he found out Motley might be looking for a new home, the coach began sending letters and telegrams inviting him to Nevada. Finally, around Christmas 1939, Aiken sent Motley's mother a telegram along with a bus ticket for Motley to head out West. Motley left South Carolina State, got his ticket, and went straight to Nevada.

CHAPTER 6

TRAGEDY OUT WEST

Things began looking up when Marion Motley arrived in Nevada. By February of 1940, the news of his outstanding talent started to spread across campus. He couldn't run from racism like he could from would-be tacklers, but Reno seemed like a place where he could focus more on football and less on people hating him because of the color of his skin.

There was racism out west, to be sure. Some people called Nevada the "Mississippi of the West" because of the racism there. Reno was a town of 21,000 where 95 percent of the residents were white. It wasn't hard to spot Motley on campus. But the racism in Nevada was not nearly as deadly as it was in the South, and the campus community welcomed Motley.

A few factors likely worked in Motley's favor. First, Washoe County, where Reno is located, was the largest county in Nevada in 1940 with a population of 32,476. The county also had the largest Black population at 284. Progressive? Not really. There were still places where Blacks knew they didn't belong or couldn't go. Reno's downtown casinos barred Blacks, and Black entertainers had to stay elsewhere. However, Reno was among the few places in the state where Black families could get a mortgage to buy houses or properties.

The other key for Motley was that he was playing for a coach in Jimmy Aiken who despised racism and would not tolerate it on his team.

As the winter of 1940 turned to spring, Motley was feeling good about his future out West. That March he and two friends from school decided to take a road trip. Reno is in the northwest corner of the state, just 10 miles from the California border. Motley wanted to experience some California sunshine.

The University of Nevada (shown in recent years) offered Marion Motley a fresh start. The school proved to be an unlikely haven for Black players in the years that followed.

Motley and his friends headed toward San Francisco. About three hours into the trip, Motley was driving on a two-lane highway near Fairfield, California, when he attempted to pass another car. It was a tragic mistake. Motley's car struck an oncoming car head-on. All six people involved—the three in Motley's car, and three in the other car—were taken to the hospital.

Motley separated a shoulder in the crash but avoided more serious injury. One of the passengers in the other car, Tom K. Nobori, a 60-year-old businessman, suffered a fractured skull. Several days later, Nobori died of pneumonia. Reports from the time didn't specify whether the pneumonia was connected to the crash, though it stands to reason the two factors were connected. Motley originally had been charged with reckless driving. However, after Nobori's death that was upgraded to the more serious charge of negligent homicide.

So many lives were changed that day. Nobori's family lost a beloved man. And even though it was an accident, the harsh reality was that a man died, and Motley had been involved. Had Motley still been in the South, who knows what would have come of this. Once again, though, Motley found some good fortune in Nevada.

The University of Nevada campus and community came out to show its love and support for Motley. He was in a Solano County jail awaiting sentencing as donations poured in from fraternities, sororities, and various student and campus organizations. But the most heartfelt contribution came from a local fifth-grader named L. J. Savage, who was a mascot for a softball team in the Reno area. He made his way to the University of Nevada, presumably with help from an adult, and offered a dollar, his entire savings, to the fund to help Motley. "I think Marion is a fine fellow, and all us kids hope nothing happens to him," Savage said. Afterward, the athletic department's Block N Society, which helps to connect students and alumni, elected the young boy as its mascot and gave him a lifetime card.

The support may have helped Motley, because he was able to leave Solano County jail and return to Reno to await his trial that was scheduled for late October. In the meantime, Motley finally got a chance to do what he loved most: play football.

Locals were eagerly awaiting the football season and an opportunity to see their new star running back. One reporter, Ty Cobb, even wrote in August 1940, a month before the start of the season: "The giant, colored lad's prowess is already rumored up and down the coast and he will be a marked man."

Nevada opened the 1940 season on September 21, hosting San Francisco State. The Wolf Pack won 47–0, with Motley carrying the ball 13 times for 90 yards and two touchdowns. Motley also played linebacker on defense, and he was just as physical on that side of the ball. But it was at running back where he was most effective. It didn't take the *Nevada State Journal* newspaper long to describe Motley as "one of the most sensational halfbacks in (school) history."

On the following Saturday, Nevada traveled to Provo, Utah, to play Brigham Young. A steady rain fell throughout the game, and neither team was able to generate much offense in a 6–6 tie. Though Motley didn't find the end zone this time, his play made an impression on Jimmy Hodgson, a *Salt Lake Tribune* reporter covering the game. Describing Motley as a "husky Negro," Hodgson called him "one of the hardest running backs to appear in Utah for some time." Another writer, Bill Coltrin, noted that

Motley's "work on defense was more outstanding than his ball carrying or passing. He was having a lot of trouble hanging onto the wet ball and never really had a chance to show his stuff because the Wolves were on defense most of the time."

The next week, at home against Idaho Southern (now Idaho State), Motley had two interceptions and returned one for a touchdown in a 62–0 win. Next up was a 78–0 win over Arkansas A&M (now Arkansas State). This time Motley scored two rushing touchdowns and threw a touchdown pass. Then, in a game at Eastern New Mexico, Motley was dominant in a 47–6 win. Among his 131 rushing yards that day were 80 on a single touchdown run. He added a score on a 15-yard run, too.

Unable to stop the running back with their bodies, the Eastern New Mexico players turned to overt racism to try to bring Motley down. Their antics were chronicled in a column by Cobb of the *Nevada State Journal* on October 28, 1940:

> *Yesterday, I heard certain remarks from the New Mexico players that were a direct insult to a man of Motley's race. Yes, they were shouted so loudly that I heard them in my seat. I was furious myself and I watched Motley closely to see his reaction, and he seemed absolutely unconcerned. I noticed intentional piling up on the big fellow. The officials doled out one penalty for that offense, but they should have called many more.*
>
> *The only noticeable effect on Motley was that he played a little harder, and instead of side-stepping players, he bowled them over and when he tackled a ball carrier he hit ferociously.*

Motley told a similar story years later to Nevada's Oral History Program. "They called us names and everything, and I just wouldn't even talk to them," he said. "If I caught one in my way, I ran over him. I ran smack over him. . . . We got a lot of respect that way."

Nevada was off to a great start with a 4–0–1 record, and Motley had proved to be a dangerous rushing threat. From there, however, the season took a downward turn. First, Motley had to face his punishment for the fatal car crash that spring. Three days after the Eastern New Mexico game, Motley was convicted of negligent homicide. He spent the next week and a half in a California jail awaiting sentencing. With their star back out, the Wolf Pack fell 7–6 at Fresno State.

Cobb, a white man who seemed to be empathetic to Motley, wrote several pieces around this time chronicling the support Motley received while taking on his legal troubles. In a November 5, 1940, article Cobb wrote, "University of Nevada students are making an unselfish effort on behalf of one of their own fellow collegians Marion Motley, the popular colored fresh-man youth, who will learn his fate on November 12. Organizations and individuals volunteered their services, and Block N, the society of athletic winners, stepped forward first and offered $50 from their treasury. More power to you, fellows."

Also, in a series of articles around this time, Cobb featured a person he referred to as "Old Grad," (Cobb didn't want to reveal his identity) who was an influential member of the university community. Old Grad wanted to make it clear to Cobb, and the Reno community, that Motley had support from the student body and alumni with clout and stature.

Cobb interviewed Old Grad about the football season, and

then shifted the conversation to a more serious tome. "I'm more concerned right at the moment with the fate of Marion Motley than I am with the loss of the Fresno game," Old Grad told Cobb. "All week I've been thinking of that poor kid sitting in a cell down in California after that terrible ordeal at which he heard himself adjudged guilty of negligent homicide. I bet the hours seemed like weeks to him and the thought that he may have to spend considerable more at San Quentin is more than enough to drive any man crazy, let alone a straightforward harmless boy whose most remote thought never included hurting anyone. My heart bleeds for that poor kid.

"The fact that Marion might never make an appearance on Mackay Field is unimportant at the moment," Old Grad continued telling Cobb. "Lord knows his past performances have given us all enough pleasant memories. The main thing is he is a student at the University of Nevada who has conducted himself in a manner to be a credit to his school and to the entire state of Nevada."

At the time, Motley's future was uncertain, with a very real chance that he would be trading in his football uniform for jailhouse attire. However, there was a ray of hope for Motley. In California, a person convicted of negligent homicide could avoid a prison sentence and be placed on probation if he or she paid a $500 fine and $500 restitution to the family. Of course, Motley did not have that kind of money. Once again, the community stepped up.

The students, faculty, fraternities, and fans at Nevada started a fundraising effort for Motley. Then, a group of important people, including the Reno chief of police and the secretary of the Reno Chamber of Commerce, went to California for Motley's sentencing to appear as character witnesses on his behalf. Though racism had by no means disappeared in Nevada, the people there seemed to genuinely like and care about Motley.

Ultimately Motley avoided jail time. He was placed on three years' probation but had to repay the $1,000 raised to keep him out of jail. In a statement published in the *Nevada State Journal*, Motley said, "I cannot tell you in words how grateful I am for what you have done for me. I shall try to show it by the quality of schoolwork I do and the service I can render on behalf of the University of Nevada and the people of this state."

Jarrett Bell, a longtime NFL columnist for *USA Today*, called the local effort to support Motley "an incredible story." That Motley's crash happened to take place in progressive California might have given him a second chance. Had it happened somewhere else? "There's no telling. We probably wouldn't have ever heard of Marion Motley," Bell said. "Had something like that occurred in South Carolina with the system there and Jim Crow laws, Motley probably would have been sentenced to be buried under the jail.

"When you think about all of the tragedies that you hear occurred in the Deep South, where people were convicted and even sentenced to death without having a fair trial . . . there was a stroke of good fortune for Marion Motley. As sad as it is that there was a tragedy that occurred that someone lost their life, for (Motley) not to lose his life and his career after that was some sort of miracle."

Larry Phillips, the Ohio sports historian, said Motley must have made a huge impression on the people in Nevada with his character. "This wasn't a group of people who fell in love with just Motley's athletic ability," he said.

Motley was able to return to the team ahead of its seventh game, a November 16 meeting at Idaho. After such a promising start of the season, the end was awful. Coming off the loss at Fresno State earlier in the month, the Wolf Pack was then shut out 6–0 at Idaho before losing 24–6 at home to Pacific and then closing out the season with a 30–7 loss at San Jose State.

All the adversity surrounding the fatal car crash and the subsequent legal issues started to take a toll. During the Idaho game, Aiken got into a physical altercation with Idaho coach Ted Bank. The reason? Bank told Aiken before the game that he was not allowed to play Motley. Bank didn't give a reason, but Aiken knew why. Bank did not want Motley to play because he was Black.

At that moment, a fight nearly broke out between Aiken and Bank. Aiken was standing up for Motley no matter what. Motley defended his coach, too. "I had to grab Jim and pick him up around the waist and hold him off the ground," Motley said years later. "He was going to punch this guy (Bank) in the mouth." A compromise was made, and Motley was permitted to play in the second half. However, sitting Motley out of the first two quarters was enough to help give Idaho a 6–0 victory in wet and icy conditions.

Motley didn't even get to play a half against Fresno State and Pacific. Those schools and Nevada had been members of the Far West Conference when a rule was implemented that barred transfer players from taking part in varsity competition within their first year at a new school. Even though all three schools were no longer in the FWC, they decided to honor the rule since it was in place when all three teams were in the conference.

What once looked like a promising first season for Motley and the Wolf Pack had quickly unraveled into a 4–4–1 record. Not all was negative, though. Aiken was a popular coach, and fans had seen what Motley could do on the field even in the face of so many challenges. Given everything Motley and the Wolf Pack went up against in 1940, there was reason to believe the next year could be much better.

CHAPTER 7

WOLF PACK DAYS IN NEVADA

Other than Historically Black College and Universities, most college football programs around the country were reluctant to sign Black players, if they did at all. Going into 1941, Nevada had three Black players on the team, including Marion Motley. Though they were reportedly treated with respect by their teammates and coaching staff, their opponents made sure to treat them with as much disrespect as possible. "Rival players intimidated and battered us, and referees often didn't call obvious fouls on them," Motley once told the *Reno Gazette-Journal*. "We were determined not to fight. The way I dealt with the intimidator was if I caught one in my way, I just ran him over."

Any hopes of Motley turning Nevada into a powerhouse proved premature. After his legal troubles in 1940, injuries limited Motley in 1941 as the team went 3–5–1. However, Motley did show some flashes of the great pro player he would become. He scored two touchdowns—one on a 66-yard run—in a 32–0 home shutout of Cal Poly-San Luis Obispo in the season opener. Where he really shined, though, was against San Jose State. Coming back from his injuries, Motley made two key plays to help secure a 20–19 win. On one, Motley ran 63 yards for a touchdown. But it was a 105-yard kickoff return for a touchdown that went down in Nevada history. Graham Gorman, a Reno banker who filmed Wolf Pack games in the early 1940s, still talked about the touchdown decades later.

"The ball bounced into the end zone around the goal posts," Gorman said, referring to the posts that were on the goal line, rather than the back of the end zone, back then. "Motley reached for it, bobbled it, picked it up again, and took off down the middle. He reversed direction at about the 20, leaped over some Spartans, knocked down two more with straight-arms before heading to the end zone. He probably covered 150 to 170 yards by the time he reached the goal line." One of the unfortunate souls who got in Motley's way was San Jose State player Lilio Marcucci. He later told the *Gazette-Journal*, "I was rendered unconscious."

In addition to playing on both sides of the ball for the Wolf Pack football team, Motley also tried a few other sports around this time. He played on the varsity basketball team. In April 1941, Motley boxed in the Reno Golden Gloves tournament, losing a decision to John Ebarb, that year's California Golden Gloves champ. And in July 1941, when the famed Kansas City Monarchs of baseball's Negro Leagues came to Reno to play a local team in an exhibition game, Motley pitched five innings for the Monarchs, giving up four hits and one run. That Monarchs team featured Satchel Paige and Buck O'Neil, though neither of those Hall of Famers played in the game.

By late September 1942, Motley was back on the football field for his final college season. After a strong finish to 1941, Motley mostly sat out the season opener, an 18–0 home win over Cal Poly, due to a sprained ankle. It was the start of an up-and-down season. Still playing on both sides of the ball—or three sides, if you count special teams—Motley took an interception 95 yards for a touchdown the next Saturday at San Francisco, then kicked the extra point. The *Nevada State Journal* compared Motley's break-away speed during that play to that of Whirlaway, the 1941 Triple Crown–winning racehorse. "He pulled away so fast it looked like (the USF defender) was standing still," the paper reported. However, those proved to be Nevada's only points in a 27–7 loss.

After a home loss to St. Mary's the next week, Motley's last great game for the Wolf Pack came in Week 4. The team from Stockton Motor Base in California came to Reno only for Motley to almost singlehandedly beat them. Motley rushed for four touchdowns and kicked three extra points in the 33–0 win.

Motley scored all of Nevada's points in another win the next week. However, this time they all came on one play: a 20-yard field goal with 90 seconds remaining. Nevada beat the Santa Ana Air Force Base 3–0. The lack of offense in that game was a sign of things to come. Though the 220-pound Motley continued to be a force as a rusher, and an increasingly dangerous passer, the Wolf Pack scored zero points in their next two games—a tie and a loss. A 14–0 home win over UC Davis on November 11 marked the end of Motley's college career. With a record of 4–3–1 in 1942, the Wolf Pack recorded their only winning record during Motley's three seasons there.

Motley's football career at Nevada was stellar, even with nagging ankle and knee injuries during his final two seasons. A gifted athlete, Motley also could have been a standout in other sports. He was an outstanding basketball player and baseball pitcher. He could sprint with the best of them on the track and was a competitive weightlifter, too. Unfortunately, no one got a chance to see him excel in those sports like he did on the football field.

For as well as he played football, Motley could never match that success in the classroom. Motley's biggest problem at Nevada was staying academically eligible. It seemed Motley would often fall asleep in class. He said he just needed more sleep than everyone else—12 to 13 hours. As a result, Motley never got to fulfill a varsity season in any of those other sports. A physical education major, he would do the work in the classroom needed to be eligible for football, then fall behind and lose his eligibility for winter and spring sports. That cycle played out throughout Motley's entire academic career at Nevada. After being declared ineligible for basketball in January 1943, Motley officially left the school.

In Nevada, Motley had met Eula May Coleman, and in February 1942, when Motley was 21 and Coleman 22, the two married. Now a year later with his wife and young son Ronald, the first of three boys the couple had, the family packed up the car and headed an hour north to Herlong, California, where Motley had accepted a job at the Sierra Army Depot.

CHAPTER 8

FOOTBALL IN THE NAVY

Marion Motley's collegiate football career came to an end during a unique time in the world—and in football. World War II had begun in 1939 in Europe, when Motley was in South Carolina. Two years later, in December 1941, the United States entered the war. A little more than a year later, Motley and his young family arrived at the army base in Herlong.

Even though he was ruled academically ineligible, Motley didn't have to leave Nevada. He could have made up the work and still had one year of eligibility remaining to play college football. The way he saw it, though, he was going to end up in the service one way or another. That he ended up working on a military base in Herlong was coincidental, but he didn't plan to stay in any one place for too long. Eventually Motley, his wife, and their young son moved back to his parents' house in Canton.

"I had a year of eligibility left, and then the service was after me," Motley said. "I said, 'Well, you can get me at my mother's house.'" The Motleys stayed in Canton for about a year, with Marion working at Republic Steel. "That's when the service grabbed me," he said. It was time to enlist.

More than 2.5 million Black men registered for the draft during World War II. Early on, they worked behind the fighting lines driving supply trucks, maintaining war vehicles, and in other support roles. By the end of the war, Black soldiers were serving on the front lines as fighter pilots, tank operators, ground troops, and officers.

Motley went an hour north to Cleveland to register. It was there that fate intervened. Around 100 men stood in line ahead of Motley. As each one stepped forward, the military commander would announce where he was headed. "Army!" the supervisor would tell one future soldier and wave him to one side. "Navy!" he would tell the next, and wave him to the other side.

When it was Motley's turn, the supervisor instead came back with a question: "Army or Navy?" Motley had to do some quick thinking; this decision could affect his life forever. "Navy," Motley called back.

For such a consequential decision, his reasoning wasn't particularly well thought out. "I heard the Navy was much cleaner, you know, and as far as eating, you got the best food with the Navy," Motley explained later. "And I had heard in the Navy, they go from one port to another. You would get off (the ship) and see the world. This was my thinking."

Motley enlisted in the U.S. Navy on Christmas Day 1944. Had he chosen to go to the army instead, he may have never played professional football. Why? Fate.

Twelve years older than Motley, Paul Brown was born on September 7, 1908, in Norwalk, Ohio, which is between Cleveland and Toledo. Nobody could have imagined how their stories would become intertwined in the years to come.

Brown's formative years came farther south in Massillon, where he starred as the Washington High School quarterback before going off to study at Ohio State and then Miami University. By the time Brown and Motley's paths first crossed in the late 1930s, Brown was back at Massillon Washington as the hotshot young head coach while Motley was the elite fullback for the team's biggest rival, Canton McKinley.

Brown's teams got the better of Motley's during those days, though that was true of almost everyone—Massillon had an 80–8–2 record under Brown from 1932 to 1940, with his teams winning six consecutive state championships and four national scholastic championships. Brown eventually left the high school ranks and became the head coach at Ohio State from 1941–43, coaching the Buckeyes to the national championship in his second season.

Before Brown could coach a fourth season, his number was called in the draft and, at age 35, he was commissioned a lieutenant in the Navy. The Ohio State coach was sent to the Great Lakes Naval Training Station near Chicago. While the war was raging in Europe and the Pacific, Brown was given a less dangerous job. Military leaders put him in charge of the Great Lakes Navy Bluejackets, a football team intended to boost morale by competing against other service teams and college programs. In what Ohio State expected to be a sabbatical before its head coach eventually returned to Columbus, Brown took his winning ways to the Bluejackets.

Motley happened to be assigned to that same Great Lakes Naval Training Center. Brown certainly remembered Motley from their days in the Ohio high school league, and the coach always had great respect for the player. In Chicago, their stories truly become connected.

It took only a few days at the training station for Motley to learn that Brown was there and coaching the football team. Not long after that, Motley discovered that he was going to be transferred to California with hundreds of others in preparation to be sent overseas. In a panic, Motley quickly found a phone and called Brown.

"Don't you move," Brown told him. "You stay right at that phone."

Brown made a call to the head of the base, as Motley remembered it. The coach said that if the Navy wanted Brown to coach the Bluejackets football team, they better stop Motley and any other football player that comes through the training center and send them to Brown. The coach called Motley back a few minutes later and told him to get his gear off the train and take it back to the barracks. "About five or 10 minutes later, the phone rings and a boatsman answers and says, 'Hey Motley, some fool on the telephone says he's the commandant of Great Lakes.' I picked up the phone and the voice said, 'Seaman First Class Motley, this is the commandant of Great Lakes.' Paul had talked to him."

Being in Chicago allowed Motley a chance to play football again, and to do so under an esteemed coach. However, the 1945 Great Lakes team got off to a terrible start. After Brown had led the team to a 9–2–1 record in 1944, the Bluejackets began 0–4–1 in 1945. Opponents outscored them 103–20, with the worst showing being a 35–0 drubbing against a team of collegiate all-stars in the season opener.

Better times were coming, though. Allied forces had landed in Normandy on June 6, 1944—D-Day—setting in motion the final push to claim victory in Europe. By the summer of 1945, the Germans had surrendered, and the Allies were closing in on Japan. With the war winding down overseas, the Bluejackets got an infusion of talent as soldiers returned home.

The Bluejackets eventually played 11 games that season against collegiate and other military teams. After the winless start, they defeated Marquette 37–27 on October 20 to begin a dominant second half of the season. Four more wins sent the team into the finale on December 1 against Notre Dame. The Fighting Irish were ranked No. 5 in the country. In what would be the Bluejackets' final game ever, 23,000 fans showed up to cheer them on at Ross Field on the Naval Station.

As described in the Notre Dame football yearbook from 1945, "Marion Motley, the sensational negro fullback, hit the N. D. line three times, crossing the goal on the last try." A missed extra point left the Bluejackets up 6–0. Though the Irish came back to take a 7–6 lead, the game soon turned into a Great Lakes rout. On one play in the fourth quarter, Motley "escaped the grasping arms of five Notre Dame tacklers" as he ran 44 yards for a touchdown, the yearbook reported. The Great Lakes Navy Bluejackets ended their four-year run with a dominating 39–7 win over one of college football's most storied teams.

Mike Brown, Paul Brown's son, was a little boy when his dad coached Motley at Great Lakes Naval Training Station. He remembered that victory mainly because Motley was so spectacular. "Motley was more than Notre Dame could handle," Mike Brown recalled. "He ran right over top of Notre Dame."

Motley also ran over Paul Brown, inadvertently, earlier in the season. Brown was a no-nonsense coach. One day, while addressing his team in the middle of the field after practice, Brown stepped back but, not realizing Motley was there, stepped on his foot. Motley, all 230 pounds of him, instinctively pushed Brown to the ground.

Everyone was shocked, to say the least. Had Motley really just put his hands on the coach? Motley later explained that his reaction was escalated due to a toe injury he had suffered in an earlier game.

"Paul backed up and stepped on my toe," Motley recalled. "I hit him in the middle of the back and boy, he flew across the surface. He said, 'What did you hit me for?' I said, 'You stepped on my foot, my sore foot.' And he just turned around and laughed. He'll tell you, 'Don't step on Motley's feet, because he'll hit you.'"

CHAPTER 9

HERE COME THE BROWNS

Black Americans could fight in the war for their country, but when the war ended in 1945 and they returned to the United States, little had changed for them. Racism was still prevalent in America. The same Jim Crow laws that codified segregation in the South were still on the books. Black soldiers who put their lives on the line for their country came home to the same discrimination they faced before they left.

Paul Brown, meanwhile, was supposed to return to Ohio State and resume his tenure as head coach. That did not happen. Pro football was in a crisis during the war. More than 600 NFL players served in the armed forces between 1941 and 1945. This exodus of talent led to turmoil within the league, including the infamous Phil-Pitt Steagles when the depleted Philadelphia Eagles and Pittsburgh Steelers had to combine their rosters in 1943, and the 1944 team known as Card-Pitt that combined the Chicago Cardinals and Steelers.

Amid all of this, Arch Ward, the influential sports editor of the *Chicago Tribune*, saw an opening. In September 1944, Ward proposed a new eight-team professional football league that would compete against the well-established NFL after the war ended. The league, called the All-America Football Conference, or AAFC, would debut in 1946.

Joe Horrigan, a past executive director of the Pro Football Hall of Fame and an NFL historian, said the upstart league outmaneuvered the established one. At the time, NFL team officials figured the players would return to their teams or enter the NFL Draft upon returning home. Ward had other ideas. "He actually started signing players for the AAFC teams in 1945 while many of them were still in the military serving in World War II," Horrigan said. "When they came out of the service, they immediately reported to those teams."

The AAFC caught the NFL flat-footed in another key spot. Arthur McBride, who was nicknamed "Mickey," was a successful businessman, having made his name first as a newspaper executive before embarking on other ventures. McBride eventually ended up in Cleveland, where he owned a printing company, in addition to taxicab companies in Cleveland, Akron, and Canton. Though not much of a football fan, he started to take an interest in the sport when his son, Arthur Jr., was a student at Notre Dame. The sport intrigued McBride, and in 1942, he decided to buy his own NFL franchise. Cleveland had a young NFL team at the time in the Rams, so McBride offered to buy it. Dan Reeves, the Rams' owner, refused to sell. But when the new eight-team AAFC league was formed, McBride jumped at the opportunity to own a team in that league. In 1944, he bought one of the AAFC's charter teams. Just like that, Cleveland now had an NFL and an AAFC team.

Next McBride needed a coach. Not knowing much about the

sport or how to own a team, he reached out to Cleveland *Plain Dealer* sportswriter John Dietrich. The writer suggested a popular and innovative young coach who was leading the Great Lakes Navy Bluejackets in Chicago: Paul Brown.

McBride took Dietrich's advice and offered Brown $17,500 a year to serve as coach and general manager of his new team. That salary, approximately $260,000 in 2022 dollars, was the largest for any football coach at any level at the time. And that wasn't all. McBride also offered Brown an ownership stake in the team as well as a stipend while he finished his tenure at the Great Lakes Naval Training Station. Brown accepted the offer.

McBride's pursuit of Brown signaled his ambitions for the team. The new coach was given free rein to put together the strongest roster possible, and he did just that, signing future Hall of Fame tackle/placekicker Lou "the Toe" Groza, wide receiver Dante Lavelli, and quarterback Otto Graham. They were paid $7,500 a year, about $113,965 in 2022 dollars. In fact, the team had so much talent that Brown wanted to keep on reserve several promising players who did not make the team's official roster. McBride made this happen by putting the reserves on his payroll as taxi drivers, although none of them were asked to drive cabs. This group came to be known as the "taxi squad," a term that is known now as the "practice squad," composed of a limited number of players who practice with the team without taking up spots on the official roster.

Around this time McBride also held a fan contest to name the team. As if it wasn't clear enough that this was Paul Brown's team, the fans voted to name it the Cleveland Browns.

Officials at Ohio State were upset to learn that Brown had

accepted the AAFC job, thinking the coach would be returning to coach the Buckeyes after the war. The opportunity to coach a professional team in Cleveland, along with the handsome amount of money, was too good for Brown to pass up.

***

The Great Lakes Navy Bluejackets' final season wrapped up in December 1945. By then, World War II had ended, with the Germans surrendering in May and Japan following that September. Marion Motley had planned to return to Nevada in 1946. As long as he took care of his academic issues, he had one year of eligibility remaining with the Wolf Pack. But when Motley, then 26 years old, heard that Brown had taken charge of a new professional football team in Cleveland, he wrote the coach a letter asking to try out. The offer was rebuffed. "He wrote me back and told me that he had all the backs he needed," Motley said later.

Figuring that was his last chance to try out for the new Cleveland team, Motley continued with his plan to head back to Nevada. "As a matter of fact," Motley said, "I had just got the tickets from my coach (Jimmy Aiken) to go back to school. He had sent me the train ticket and everything to go back."

That Brown turned down Motley wasn't entirely unexpected in the mid-1940s. With the war over, white servicemen were able to resume their previous lives. For some, that meant returning to college or professional football in the NFL. But turning pro wasn't an option for Motley and other Blacks. They returned home to segregation and inequality, and the NFL was no exception. While the league never codified a rule against signing Black players, the NFL—like Major League Baseball—was operating under a "gentleman's agreement" among owners. No team had signed a Black player since 1933.

Wheels were in motion to begin changing that in both sports, though. Excluding Black players was not just discriminatory but also bad business. Teams were voluntarily depriving themselves of talented players. Brown recognized this, and he decided he wasn't going to follow the status quo. He was going to sign the best players, regardless of their race.

Though Motley was turned away, Brown did invite a different Black player to try out: his former Ohio State lineman Bill Willis. At the time, Willis was considering an option to try out for the Montreal Alouettes, a new team starting in 1946 in Canada. "Actually, he was on his way there when he indirectly got a message from Paul Brown," his son Bill Willis Jr. said. The message came via a sportswriter in Columbus. "(He) said, 'You might want to show up at the Browns' training camp,'" Willis Jr. said. With that, Bill Willis changed his plans and headed for Bowling Green, Ohio.

A Columbus native, Willis had already broken barriers at his hometown university. A two-way player, he helped Ohio State win the 1942 national title, then became the school's first Black All-American in 1943 and 1944. Though he was considered small for a defensive tackle, at only 210 pounds, he made up for it with his quickness. As Brown wrote in his 1979 memoir *PB: The Paul Brown Story*: "He often played as a middle or nose guard on our five-man defensive line, but we began dropping him off the line of scrimmage a yard because his great speed and pursuit carried him to the point of attack before anyone would block him. Bill was the forerunner of the modern middle linebacker."

Once training camp started, Willis dominated, disrupting the Browns' offensive unit led by future Hall of Fame quarterback Otto Graham. "Everybody got knocked down," center Mo Scarry once told *USA Today* NFL columnist Jarrett Bell. "We used to just line up over the ball and snap it. With Willis, though, you had to put the ball as far as you could out in front of you, to get as far away from him as you could. He changed the whole way we snapped the ball." Willis made the team and signed a contract for $4,000. Ten days later, Brown invited Motley to try out.

The reasons for Brown's change of heart about Motley remain a source of speculation. Motley's son Raymond felt Brown only brought his dad into training camp to room with Willis. Willis had a strong relationship with Brown, but the thinking goes that the Browns needed a second Black player to room with Willis during training camp. That would line up with Motley's

Despite his smaller frame, Bill Willis became a two-way star at Ohio State, earning All-America honors in 1943 and 1944. That was a first for a Black player at the school.

recollection of events. The actual call to invite Motley to try out came from John Brickels, one of Brown's assistants. "He asked me if I would like to come up and try out for the football team," Motley said, "because Willis had made the ball club and they had to have someone to go along with—they wanted another colored guy." Motley, who was back working at Republic Steel ahead of his planned return to Reno, said he was asked to be in Bowling Green the next afternoon, so a relative drove him to training camp.

Mike Brown, who went on to become an NFL executive himself and now owns the Cincinnati Bengals, disputes that was his father's intention. "I've heard that story. I've always thought it was apocryphal," he said. "I never asked my dad. All I know is they (Willis and Motley) both were there at camp very quickly together, and they were roommates, but Marion's the one that came up with that story. I think it must've been a good after-dinner joke. . . . I don't think that's so. I think he was brought on because my dad knew he was a tremendous player and wanted him for the team."

At a Browns banquet years later, Paul Brown told his version of these events. "It was a little touchy situation at the time," he said. "I called up a couple of my friends, one here in Canton and one in Columbus. I had them gather together Bill Willis and Marion Motley, and I said, 'Now you send them over to Bowling Green . . . and tell them to walk in and ask me for a tryout.' I said, 'I'll handle it from there.' And you know what happened? They both became not only great players but great leaders. They were integral cogs in our machine for many, many years to come. I've never known two people that I respected any more in my years of football."

CHAPTER 10

BREAKING THE LINE

The game of football dates to November 6, 1869, when the school now known as Rutgers University defeated Princeton University 6–4 in New Brunswick, New Jersey. By 1892, the sport had been professionalized, with the Allegheny Athletic Association paying guard William "Pudge" Heffelfinger $500 to play in a game against the rival Pittsburgh Athletic Club. As with baseball, Blacks weren't always barred from the pro game. Charles Follis, a halfback, signed in 1904 with a team in Shelby, Ohio, making him the first known Black pro football player.

Fritz Pollard was perhaps the most notable Black player in the sport's early days. An elusive, 5'9" and 165-pound back out of Brown University, he joined the fittingly named Akron Pros in 1919. When the team joined the upstart American Professional Football Association the next year, Pollard became one of two Black players in the league, leading the Pros to an undefeated season and to what's now recognized as the first NFL championship. A year after that, while still playing, Pollard became the NFL's first Black coach when Akron named him co-coach. The Pro Football Hall of Fame recognized his contributions as "the

Fritz Pollard was one of two Black players in the NFL's first season in 1920. A feared halfback, Pollard also coached four NFL teams between 1920 and 1926.

most feared running back in the fledgling league" when enshrining him in the Class of 2005.

"It was evident in my first year at Akron back in 1919 that they didn't want blacks in there getting that money," Pollard is quoted as saying on the HOF website. "And here I was, playing and coaching and pulling down the highest salary in pro football."

It wouldn't last. In 1933, when the contracts of Black players Joe Lillard and Ray Kemp were up, the league made its move. Though never codified in writing, the team owners, led by openly racist Boston Redskins owner George Preston Marshall, agreed to not sign any Black players for the 1934 season. That "gentleman's agreement" lasted until 1946.

In the weeks before Paul Brown brought Bill Willis and Marion Motley into his new Cleveland team, a movement was underway in Los Angeles. A decade before the Dodgers came to town, bringing major league baseball to the West Coast, pro football arrived in Southern California.

Since their founding in 1937, the Cleveland Rams had enjoyed a mostly losing existence. After seven straight seasons without a winning record, things finally came together in 1945, when rookie quarterback Bob Waterfield led the team to a 9–1 record and, ultimately, the city's first NFL championship. By then it was already too late. A popular young coach was putting together a new pro team for the northern Ohio city. Rams owner Dan Reeves, already struggling financially in Cleveland, was reportedly "anxious" about the situation. Rather than trying to compete against Paul Brown and his new AAFC team, Reeves packed up and moved the Rams to Los Angeles.

A big city, but not yet the metropolis that it is today, Los Angeles had a sporting tradition—it had hosted the 1932 Summer Olympics, after all—but had never fielded a professional team in one of the country's major leagues. Before the Rams took the field there, though, Reeves faced an ultimatum. Since NFL owners had implemented their gentleman's agreement, teams had lived by their commitment to shun Black players.

Black activists and sportswriters, led by former Negro Leagues baseball player Halley Harding, then writing for the *Los Angeles Tribune*, demanded that if Reeves wanted to move his team to the Los Angeles Coliseum, a taxpayer-supported facility, he should have to integrate and sign Black players. Desperate for a stadium, Reeves ultimately agreed. On January 23, 1946, the Los Angeles Coliseum Commission approved use of the 103,000-seat stadium for the Rams' Sunday home games. The following March, the Rams lived up to their end of the agreement by signing half-back Kenny Washington, a former UCLA standout. End Woody Strode, another former UCLA Bruin, followed in May.

A few months after the Rams signed Strode and Washington, the Browns brought in Willis. Motley would eventually become the fourth member of the group that would reintegrate major American professional sports. First, though, he had to get through training camp.

Browns training camp had already been going on for 10 days when Motley arrived. At 6'1" and around 230 pounds, he was bigger than most linemen. Compared with the rest of the full-backs, Motley was in another league athletically. Whenever they ran sprints, Motley charged out front. In everything he did, he was head and shoulders above the competition.

On Motley's second day, Brown put him on the first team.

Years later, Motley explained that he could feel tension and jealousy from the other fullbacks after that. He had already arrived at camp more than a week late. Now he was taking over the position.

Motley wasn't looking for special treatment, though. He wanted to earn his job. Brown sensed what was going on as well. "I guess the good Lord had the halo over Paul's head and told him to move me back to fourth team," Motley said. "Everybody was happy after that."

Once the first scrimmage began, though, there was no doubt who should be the starting fullback. Motley ran over everyone. One teammate described him as being like a wrecking ball. After the game, someone asked Bill Willis, "What was the matter with (Motley)? Was he mad tonight?" Willis responded, "No, he's just trying to make the football team." Motley showed that he had the potential to be one of the greatest running backs in the history of the sport. Finally, the team offered Motley a contract. He'd be paid $4,000—the same as Willis.

***

Racism and segregation still existed, and those things did not end when the Rams and Browns signed the Black players. At Browns training camp, Brown made it clear that any player who had an issue with Motley or Willis wasn't welcome.

"When Paul signed us, there were a few (Browns) who weren't too happy," Motley told the *Philadelphia Daily News* in October 1995. "Paul addressed that at the first meeting. He said, 'If you can't get along with our teammates, you won't be here.' He didn't have to spell it out—everyone knew what he meant. Once we began practice, the matter was settled. The other players saw that

Bill and I could help the team, so they shut their mouths. As time passed, we got to be really close. The guys would stick up for us if they saw (opponents) pulling anything dirty."

One of Motley's white teammates, Cliff Lewis, also recalled that meeting. "At first, there were some guys who said, 'I'm not going to play with those so-and-so,'" he said. "But it didn't take Paul Brown long to put an end to that. He got the guys together and said, 'Listen, these two young men can play football. If you want to win football games with them, you're welcome to join us. If not, get out.'"

In the Browns' only preseason game, a win against the Brooklyn Dodgers at the Akron Rubber Bowl on August 30, 1946, Brown turned to Gene Fekete to start at fullback. Fekete, who had won a national title with Brown at Ohio State, got the nod again on September 6 when the team made its regular-season debut. And what a debut it was.

A record crowd of more than 60,000 fans showed up at Municipal Stadium in Cleveland to see the Browns destroy the Miami Seahawks 44–0. The introduction of Brown's innovative new "T" formation offense surely helped. Motley, for his part, caught a 35-yard pass to set up a field goal.

With Fekete out due to injury the next week, Motley got the start against the Chicago Rockets. He rushed for 122 yards and a touchdown on 12 carries in the Browns' 20–6 win at Soldier Field. That's when Motley won the starting position, a position he would hold for years to come.

CHAPTER II

LIKE BROTHERS

As expected, Marion Motley and Bill Willis became "brothers," in a sense, upon joining up together with the Browns. It might have helped that the two came from similar backgrounds. Willis, like Motley, was born in Georgia, in 1921. A year after that, in 1922, Willis's family moved to Columbus, Ohio, for the same reasons as the Motleys: to escape financial hardship and the Jim Crow laws in the South.

Willis attended Columbus East High School, where he ran track and played football. As a tackle on defense and an end on offense, Willis earned honorable mention all-state honors as a senior. After high school, he planned to take a year off from school to work. However, his high school coach wrote a letter to Paul Brown, who by then had taken over as the Ohio State coach, encouraging the Buckeyes to give Willis a tryout. Willis was considered undersized for his position at 202 pounds, but he was agile as a lineman, and Brown was looking for that type of player.

Willis joined the Ohio State team in 1942 as a middle guard, or nose tackle in modern parlance. Though Willis was smaller than usual for that position, he proved to be much quicker than the centers he played across from, so he could get off the line faster to make tackles. This helped him step in right away and play a key role on one of the most important teams in program history. The Buckeyes went 9–1, won the Western Conference (now Big Ten Conference) title, and, for the first time, were named national champions after ending the season No. 1 in the Associated Press poll.

However, with U.S. involvement in World War II ramping up, several Ohio State players left school to join the military before the 1943 season. Willis volunteered for the army but because of varicose veins, a medical condition in which superficial veins in the legs become enlarged and twisted, he was available for service only in the case of a national emergency. His varicose veins didn't prevent him from playing football, though, and although the Buckeyes went 3–6 during the 1943 season, Willis was named first-team all-conference.

The war effort hit Ohio State again before the 1944 season. This time it was Brown who left Columbus, headed for the Great Lakes Naval Training Station. Under his replacement and longtime assistant Carroll Widdoes, the Buckeyes charged to a 9–0 record and a No. 2 final ranking in the AP poll. Willis was again a key player in the effort. United Press International named him to its All-America team, and Willis also played in the College All-Star Game. Though the Chicago Bears defeated the College All-Stars 24–21, Willis was named the game's outstanding player.

There was little question that Willis had the skills to play football on the next level. He had two things working against him. First, at 210 pounds he was considered small, even back then. Second, and more impenetrable, was the unwritten agreement among pro football team owners to not sign Black players. With no football equivalent of baseball's Negro Leagues to continue in, Willis's career appeared over when he graduated from Ohio State in 1945.

Resigned to the fact that his playing days were over, Willis took a coaching job at Kentucky State College, an HBCU in Frankfort, Kentucky. In an interview years later, Willis admitted his heart was never really into coaching, but with no options to play professionally, coaching was his best alternative. A call from his old college coach gave his playing career new life.

According to a story on the Pro Football Hall of Fame's website, Paul Brown brought Willis in for a tryout with his fledgling Cleveland Browns in 1946. Undersized and competing against all-white teammates, Willis nonetheless lined up in the center of a five-man defensive line and then bulldozed his way to quarterback Otto Graham four straight times. When Brown finally determined that Willis was not offside, but instead just very fast, he offered his former star a contract that same day.

Willis and Motley became teammates and roommates with the Browns, but their relationship quickly went much deeper. As two rookies, both Black, trying to make their way in the otherwise all-white AAFC, they learned they could rely on each other. Jarrett Bell, the *USA Today* NFL columnist, recalled that the two players "became joined at the hip."

"When you have social situations where the players had a night off during training camp, what are they going to do? It wasn't like the white players were taking them to go to town with them," Bell said. "They were going their ways, and Motley and Willis were left to their own devices to do what they decided to do. They would do things together, like eat dinner somewhere or go to the theater."

On many occasions, Motley and Willis would just stay in their rooms and play cards. Mike Brown, who was 11 years old during that training camp in 1946 in Bowling Green, recalled the future Hall of Famers welcoming him into their circle. "I would go up to the dorms and they would let me play hearts with them. That was a favorite memory of mine," Brown said.

During their card games, the players were as competitive as they were on the football field, though Brown recalled that many times Motley would let him win just to see the elated look on his face. "I would put the queen down on Motley's cards and he would erupt like he lost the biggest game, and everyone would laugh," Brown said. "He did that for my benefit. But I remember those guys were truly kind to me, and I have wonderful memories of them, stemming from that time with them. They were my heroes as players. They were good people."

Browns teammate Dante Lavelli, a prolific cardplayer, recalled playing with Motley and Willis while the team was in California for training camp at a ranch owned by influential newspaper publisher William Randolph Hearst. "There were bunkhouses out there," Lavelli said. "We used to have to pull the shades down so (Coach) Brown wouldn't see us. . . . We used to play for nickels and dimes, and Motley and Willis were always the big winners. They used to get these big wastepaper baskets to put all their money in."

Motley and Willis became insulated, yet at the same time their friendship and bond grew strong because of it. They always had each other's backs, Bell said. Willis once explained that after games, he and Motley would go back to their rooms and compare notes about what happened in the game—what an opponent said or did to them, like stepping on their fingers with their cleats or kicking them. "One of the things that is striking from the conversations I had with Willis was him telling me about if there were situations where opposing players said things that were out of line, and typically that would happen, they knew they had teammates who saw this as well, who came to their defense," Bell said.

There was a reason why teammates had Motley and Willis's backs: Paul Brown. Motley said Brown made it clear that he would not tolerate any racism within his team. "When any of the southern (white) kids used to come to our camp, the first thing they would do when they got to camp was come and meet us," Motley said, referring to himself and Willis. "They would come and find us to shake hands and make friends with us. Somewhere along the line, they were told when they got here that they would have to get along with us or they couldn't play here."

Clem Willis said his father told him about many times when Willis and Motley would want to lash out or retaliate but knew they couldn't and shouldn't. "My father had a lot of restraint." Clem said. "He got along very well with folks just because of his niceness. And Mr. Motley was more of the backslapping, gregarious, 'We're gonna have fun' kind of guy, so they worked well together because it was them against the world. They would consult with each other, and they would just decide to run over people. They didn't want to start fights or do anything negative. They just played by the rules, played a little bit harder by the rules. They had each other's back all the time."

CHAPTER 12

STARS OF THE AAFC

The 44–0 drubbing of the Miami Seahawks set the tone for how dominating the Browns would be in the AAFC's debut 1946 season. With Otto Graham at quarterback throwing to talented ends Dante Lavelli and Mac Speedie, the team was particularly dangerous through the air. That the Browns also had one of the game's great fullbacks in Marion Motley, who could both block and bulldoze with the best of them, only made the team more unstoppable.

The AAFC was split into two divisions, with the Browns playing in the West along with the Chicago Rockets, Los Angeles Dons, and San Francisco 49ers. The Eastern Division included the Brooklyn Dodgers, Buffalo Bisons, Miami Seahawks, and New York Yankees. Early on, the West was clearly the stronger division, but that hardly mattered for the Browns. They jumped out to a 7–0 start before their first taste of adversity.

Motley turned in his best offensive performance of the season in that seventh game, rushing for 143 yards and two touchdowns in a convincing win over the Dons. Then, in back-to-back games, the Browns fell to the 49ers at home and then the Dons—the AAFC's glamour team, with Hollywood connections galore—by one point on the road. Motley was held to just 50 yards of total offense in the two games. That two-game losing streak marked perhaps the lowest point during the Browns' AAFC tenure, and it didn't last long. They then ran off five straight wins to end the season 12–2, setting up a December 22 title game against the Yankees at Cleveland Municipal Stadium.

Cleveland was easily the league's best team, and Motley proved to be a big reason why. In addition to his irreplaceable blocking for Graham, he rushed for a team-high 601 yards and five touchdowns that season, averaging an astonishing 8.2 yards per carry. New York's star rookie Spec Sanders led the league with 709 rushing yards, but his 140 carries were almost twice as many as Motley's. And that powerful rushing only complemented one of the league's strongest passing attacks led by Graham, Lavelli, and Speedie.

Cleveland came into the title game having scored 423 points and given up just 137. The 49ers ranked second in each category at 307 and 189. In fact, an argument could be made that the 9–5 49ers were the AAFC's second best team, with the Yankees having built their 10–3–1 record in part by beating up on the weaker Eastern Division, where no other team won more than three games. Nonetheless, with Sanders leading the way, the Yankees were no pushovers, and they showed that early in the championship game by intercepting Graham and turning that into a field goal to go up 3–0 in the first quarter. That set the stage for a back-and-forth battle.

The Browns answered in the second quarter, with Graham working passes to Lavelli and Speedie until they reached the Yankees' 13, at which point two handoffs to Motley finished the job and Cleveland went up 7–3. Sanders then put the visitors back on top with a short rushing touchdown in the third, and after failing the point-after conversion, New York went into the fourth quarter holding a 9–7 lead. Once again the Browns came back, though, this time on a 16-yard touchdown pass from Graham to Lavelli to secure a 14–9 win and the first AAFC title.

Cleveland's stars all came out in the win. Graham threw for 213 yards, and Lavelli (87 yards) and Speedie (71) led the team in receiving. Motley rushed for a game-high 98 yards on 13 carries, averaging 7.5 yards per carry. Meanwhile, Cleveland's defense held Sanders to just 55 yards on the ground.

No player in AAFC history rushed for as many yards as Marion Motley. He ran for 3,024 yards during 52 regular-season games from 1946–49.

The Browns remained the class of the AAFC in the years that followed. After going a league-best 12–1–1 the next season, they traveled to New York to face the Yankees for the title on December 17, 1947. Motley didn't score in the game, but he rushed for a game-high 109 yards—including a 51-yard run. Behind rushing touchdowns from Graham and halfback Edgar Jones, the Browns won 14–3.

The game was also significant for other reasons. In addition to Motley and Bill Willis, the Browns had brought in a third Black player, Horace Gillom, prior to the season. Gillom had played for Paul Brown at Massillon Washington High School and then Ohio State before ending his college career in 1946 with Nevada. Though Gillom was also used as a backup end (on offense and defense) early in his pro career, he was primarily a punter, even making a Pro Bowl during his decade with the team.

Thousands of Black fans from Harlem came out to see the three Browns players in that AAFC title game. Afterward, they rushed the field to celebrate with them.

Mike Brown was still just a kid, yet he understood how important Motley, Willis, and Gillom were to Black fans. "It mattered to the Black community in Northeast Ohio, that I know," Brown said. "I know people who were part of that community, and guys like Marion and Bill Willis gave them hope for the future. It gave them a path to the future. It gave them confidence to continue to go on and fight for a better life for themselves."

It helped, too, that they were thriving on the field, especially Motley. His third season with the Browns was his best yet. He led the league in rushing with 964 yards, which was good for nearly 70 yards per game. He added seven touchdowns, including two as a receiver. Behind his powerful running, the Browns put together what might have been their best season ever.

Through their first nine games, the Browns were a perfect 9–0. Wins had become so predictable in Cleveland that some fans started to stay home. That wasn't the case when the undefeated 49ers came to Cleveland on November 14, 1948. The crowd of 82,769 was the biggest in pro football history to that point. Despite being dubbed "the gridiron battle of the century," the game ended up being "a dull affair," the *New York Times* reported. After the teams traded touchdowns in the first quarter, Jones scored on a 4-yard rush in the third to put Cleveland up for good, 14–7. Their rematch two weeks (and three Browns games) later at San Francisco's Kezar Stadium was more dramatic. This time Motley caught a short touchdown pass in a 31–28 win. The Browns secured a perfect 14–0 regular season the following week by going up 31–0 on the Dodgers before eventually winning 31–21.

Marion Motley poses with sons Ronald, *left*, 6, and Raymond, 4, after a 1948 game.

That set up an AAFC title game three weeks later against Buffalo, who by then were called the Bills (though they are not the same team as the current Buffalo Bills). In front of slightly less than 23,000 at Municipal Stadium, Motley was dominant. He scored three of the Browns' touchdowns, including on 29- and 31-yard runs, as they destroyed the Bills 49–7. Motley's 133 rushing yards were more than twice the Bills' total. With 15 wins and no losses, those Browns became the first major pro football team to go through an entire season and playoffs without a loss or tie. Only the 1972 Miami Dolphins have matched that feat.

The Browns' unbeaten streak eventually extended to 29 games, and they went 9–1–2 on the way to a fourth straight AAFC title in 1949. Motley scored again in the championship game, this time on a 68-yard run, as the Browns made easy work of the 49ers in a 21–7 win.

Four years into the AAFC, the Browns were clearly the class of the league. They had gone 47–4–3 and won all four championships in league history. No other AAFC player rushed for more yards than Motley's 3,024, and he added 31 touchdowns—including four as a receiver and one on an interception return.

The only thing that could stop the Browns, it turned out, was the league disbanding. After a successful first two seasons, league attendance started to drop in 1948, which meant revenue for owners dropped as well. Another factor that contributed to the league folding was the growing gap between the best and worst teams.

Though the AAFC shut down, Motley and the Browns got a second chance. Heading into the 1950 season, the NFL agreed to bring on the Browns, 49ers, and Baltimore Colts (who had replaced the Seahawks in 1947). The additions weren't exactly embraced, though. Many NFL fans and executives didn't think the AAFC teams would be competitive. After all, the NFL had been around for nearly three decades by then, its teams all well established. The AAFC, on the other hand, couldn't even make it five years. How could they match up with the NFL powers? The NFL soon found out just how dominant Motley, Willis, and the Browns were.

CHAPTER 13

WELCOME TO THE NFL

I n 2019, a panel of 57 media members was asked to name the NFL's "greatest game changer." They selected Paul Brown. For as much as football has grown since Brown last roamed the sidelines in 1975, his fingerprints remain all over the game.

Upon his arrival in Cleveland in the mid-1940s, Brown hired a full-time coaching staff and revolutionized college scouting. Classroom learning, including the use of film study and playbooks, began during his tenure. He even started the trend of having his teams stay together in a hotel the night before home games.

On the field, Brown was also credited with revolutionizing passing offense—and defense. He became the first coach to call plays from the sideline, which he did by giving the call to a guard on the sideline, then having that player sub into the game and deliver the play. Brown was also influential in the development of the face mask.

"Whether they know it or not, nearly everyone in football has been affected by Paul Brown," former NFL commissioner Pete Rozelle, quite the game changer himself, was quoted as saying in an article on the Pro Football Hall of Fame's website. "His wealth of ideas changed the game."

Those innovations weren't necessarily embraced early on,

Perhaps no person influenced pro football more than Paul Brown.

however, especially when the upstart Browns arrived in the NFL. Cleveland had utterly dominated the AAFC. The NFL didn't quite roll out the red carpet for the Browns' arrival in 1950, though. What was the AAFC anyway?

"Paul was a man that reorganized professional football, no doubt," Marion Motley said in 1968. "We were the laughingstock when we came into the National Football League in 1950. We were like a high school team carrying notebooks."

Among the dismissive NFL owners, George Preston Marshall of the Washington Redskins stood out for his disrespect of Brown and his team. According to Andy Piascik, whose 2007 book *The Best Show in Football* covered this era of the Browns, Marshall said the NFL's weakest team could "toy with the Browns." As if to put an extra fine point on it, the NFL scheduled the Browns to enter the league with a visit to Philadelphia Municipal Stadium, home of the defending champion Eagles.

Brown made sure his players understood the significance of this game. He told them that everything they established during their dominance in the AAFC would mean nothing if they did not win. The pressure on the players was formidable.

The crowd of 71,237 in Philadelphia was at the time the eighth largest in professional football history. Fans didn't get to see the rout they were expecting, though. Cleveland forced the Eagles into a three-and-out on their first possession of the game, then the Browns appeared to take an early lead after a 64-yard punt return by Don Phelps. However, the touchdown was called back on a clipping penalty.

Philadelphia capitalized on the Browns' mistake, and a 17-yard field goal by Cliff Patton put the home team up 3–0. Cleveland answered with a 59-yard touchdown pass from Otto Graham to Dub Jones. With kicker Lou Groza in the locker room nursing an injured shoulder, Cleveland offensive lineman Forrest "Chubby" Grigg nailed the point after.

The Eagles then drove to Cleveland's 6-yard line, but that's when, as Rick Reilly recalled in a 1991 *Sports Illustrated* article, Brown "snuck Motley in at linebacker."

"All he did was smother the Eagles' running backs four straight times," Reilly wrote. "Offense, defense, blocking, tackling—he was a one-man demolition company."

The Eagles stayed out of the end zone, and another long pass from Graham, this time to Dante Lavelli, put Cleveland up 14–3 at halftime. The domination only continued from there. The Browns outscored the Eagles 21–7 in the second half to win 35–10. Motley rushed 11 times for 48 yards and added 26 yards on two catches.

A half-century later, Hall of Fame Eagles linebacker Chuck Bednarik recalled the game in an interview with *The Morning Call* in Allentown, Pennsylvania. On Brown's gameplan: "They did things we had never seen before," Bednarik said. "They shifted into different formations. They sent backs in motion. It did confuse us very much." Motley, the tough-as-nails linebacker said, was "like a tank."

"He was the toughest guy I'd ever had to try and tackle," Bednarik said.

But one quote might have summed it up best.

"I had nothing but the most respect for them," Bednarik said. "They were a powerhouse. That was one helluva team."

After defeating the Eagles in the opener, the Browns traveled to Baltimore and dismantled the Colts 31–0. However, the New York Giants beat Cleveland 6–0 the next week, handing the Browns their first shutout in 62 games. As it turned out, the Browns' only two losses during the 1950 season came at the hands of the Giants. They also lost 17–13 on October 22 at the Polo Grounds in New York, which put Cleveland's record at 4–2.

As the season went on, Motley found his footing as an offensive force. After putting up 233 rushing yards and a single touchdown through the first six games, he nearly matched those totals in one epic performance.

On October 29, the Browns hosted the Pittsburgh Steelers at Cleveland Municipal Stadium, marking just the second meeting between the two teams. Cleveland came into the game known for its prolific passing behind Graham. Motley upended that reputation practically on his own. The Associated Press report from the next day summed up his performance: "The big fellow went for a couple of 12-yard jaunts through the middle the first two times he had the ball, took a pitchout from Graham for 50 yards to the Steelers two, went 17 yards for a touchdown after a pitchout from Graham, zoomed 69 on a trap play for a touchdown, and rolled 20 yards for another crack at the line as he made himself generally obnoxious to the Pittsburgh team."

Motley rushed just 11 times in the game, but he picked up 188 yards and two touchdowns. His 17.09 yards per carry stood as an NFL record for decades. The 45–7 win put the Browns back on the upswing, and they stayed there with six consecutive wins to close out the season. Motley was a big reason why. Two weeks after his romp against the Steelers, Motley put up 114 rushing yards against the San Francisco 49ers, then he dropped 178 on the Redskins the next week. By the end of the season, he had piled up an NFL-best 810 rushing yards.

The regular season ended on a down note, however. In Washington for the finale on December 10, Motley accused a Redskins player of using racial slurs and fought back. Though the Browns went on to win, Motley was ejected. Though details of the incident were scarce, given the amount of racism he had to endure on the field, the slurs had to have taken a toll on Motley.

The Browns had shown they could more than compete in the NFL during the regular season. Now with a 10–2 record, they set off to do it again in the playoffs. As it worked out, they faced the NFL's only other 10–2 team—which happened to be the team that beat them twice during the regular season. Both the Browns and Giants were in the NFL's American Conference. After winning a coin toss, the Browns hosted the December 17 game on a cold Cleveland afternoon. With the field frozen and freezing wind gusts throughout the stadium, Groza proved the difference as Cleveland finally beat the Giants when it mattered most, 8–3. Groza's field goals put the Browns up 6–3 before Bill Willis sealed the win with a safety in the fourth quarter.

Going into the season, Brown had challenged his team to be fearless. The Browns had dominated the AAFC, and they could hold their own in the NFL, too. Few might have believed that, but the Browns did, and now they were hosting the NFL Championship Game on Christmas Eve at Cleveland Municipal Stadium. The city's former team, the Rams, came back to town as the opponent.

The matchup was one not lacking for intrigue. Five years after departing Cleveland for Los Angeles, the Rams were back in town and featured one of the greatest offenses the league had ever seen. A pair of future Hall of Fame quarterbacks, Bob Waterfield and Norm Van Brocklin, each started six games. With the league's top receiver in Tom Fears and another future Hall of Fame receiver in Elroy "Crazy Legs" Hirsch, the Rams averaged 309 passing yards a game, which was a record that stood until 1984. Meanwhile, running back Verda "Vitamin" Smith Jr. led a rushing attack that averaged 143 rushing yards per game.

Amidst frigid conditions once again in Cleveland, that high-powered Los Angeles offense didn't need much time to strike. On the first offensive play of the game, Waterfield threw an 82-yard touchdown pass to Glenn Davis for a 7–0 lead. The Browns had some firepower of their own, though. In addition to featuring the league's leading rusher in Motley, Cleveland's passing game also featured a trio of future Hall of Famers in quarterback Graham, and receivers Lavelli and Mac Speedie.

The Browns answered when Graham hit Dub Jones for a 27-yard touchdown catch.

Motley ended up carrying the ball just six times for nine yards in the game as passing—and Graham's scrambling—ruled the day. After Los Angeles went up 14–7 late in the first quarter, the Browns answered with a 37-yard touchdown pass from Graham to Lavelli. However, the extra-point attempt failed, and Cleveland trailed 14–13 at halftime. A 39-yard touchdown pass to Lavelli put Cleveland up in the third quarter, but this time Los Angeles answered and took a 28–20 lead into the fourth.

Needing some magic, the Browns found it with just over 10 minutes remaining. Graham dropped back and lofted the ball 14 yards downfield. It soared precisely to the back shoulder of halfback Rex Bumgardner in the left corner of the end zone. Even with a defender inches away, Bumgardner snagged the pass, then slid out of the side of end zone with the ball tightly secured. Groza's extra point cut the Rams' lead to 28–27, setting up a dramatic finish.

After a defensive stand by the Browns' defense, Graham scrambled deep into Los Angeles territory on the next possession before fumbling and giving the Rams the ball back. But after another defensive stand, Cleveland took possession once again, this time at its own 31-yard line with 1:49 remaining. Again, Graham got to work, scrambling and passing the ball to the Cleveland 11. From there, Graham took a quarterback sneak to the middle of the field to set up a possible 16-yard game-winning field-goal attempt for Groza. With the hometown crowd cheering, and hoping, Cleveland lined up.

The snap . . . the kick . . . it was . . . GOOD!

A last-ditch effort by the Rams fell short, and Cleveland held on to claim a 30–28 win and the NFL championship in its first season. It was a monumental achievement. Going into the season, no one expected the Browns to be competitive, much less win the league. Paul Brown and his players did.

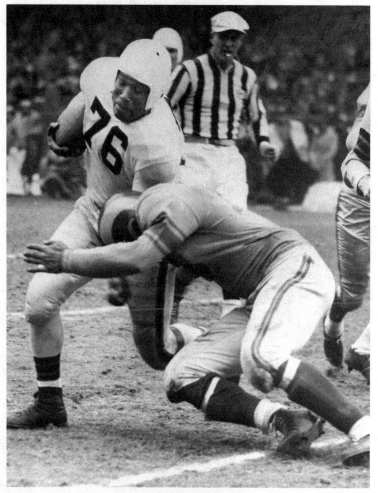

Marion Motley charges through the Los Angeles Rams' defense during the 1950 NFL title game. The Browns won 30–28 to complete their first NFL season with a championship.

CHAPTER 14

PLAYING ON

During the 1950s, it was customary that the NFL champs play against a team of college football all-stars before the start of the next season. Since the Browns were the reigning NFL champs, they would be playing in the 1951 exhibition game.

The Browns headed to Bowling Green, Ohio, for preseason. During a practice before the all-star game, Marion Motley collided with teammate Tony Adamle, injuring his knee. Motley later contended that the team trainer advised him to sit out a couple of days, but Paul Brown insisted he not miss any practice. Motley said he practiced on his injured knee and ended up seeing a doctor, who also advised rest. Motley said Brown, again, insisted that he not miss practice. Motley always felt that is how his knee worsened and shortened his career.

"Paul used to give us these fundamental drills of blocking and tackling, and this particular day I was on a reverse body block, and Tony's knee hit my knee right in the little point," Motley said. "As soon as he hit me . . . hit the nerve . . . the darn thing just hurt and ached. By the time practice ended, my knee was a balloon. We practiced and I kept practicing, running on one leg."

Motley thought he would have at least a day or two off from practice before the all-star game, but that wasn't the case. "Even

Marion Motley averaged 5.7 yards per carry throughout his career.

the team trainer thought I should have a couple days off. But Paul said, 'No! No! Let him come on out here. He can come out and run a little bit. You don't have to run around, just hop around on it.' And that's all I was doing. But see, what I did was this leg and knee was hurting, and I was running on this one and wound up with both knees full of water."

On August 17, 1951, the Browns faced the nation's best college players in the 18th annual College All-Star Game. A crowd of 92,180 fans showed up at Chicago's Soldier Field for the game. Though both teams started slowly, the Browns eventually dominated the college team, winning 33–0. Motley managed to get through that game, but just barely.

"After the game, I came out of Soldier Field and was standing up against the wall," Motley said. "They had to drive my car down into the ramp right beside me because I couldn't move. I couldn't even walk."

For the decade that lasted from 1946 to 1955, the Browns were nearly unstoppable. During that time, Cleveland played for a professional football championship every year, going 7–3 in those games. The Browns won the NFL's American and then Eastern Conference championship for six straight years from 1950 to 1955. They won NFL titles in 1950, 1954, and 1955. Arguably, no team in football history has been as good for as long as the Browns were during that stretch.

Motley's powerful, bruising play at fullback was a big reason why. He spent eight of his nine pro football seasons with the Browns, from 1946 to 1953. In 99 career games, he rushed for 4,712 yards and 31 touchdowns, while adding another 1,107 yards and seven scores as a receiver. During that time he won two rushing titles, leading the AAFC in 1948 and then the NFL in 1950. Though Motley was never quite the same after that 1951 College All-Star Game, at his best he was simply one of the greatest runners the game has ever known.

As a running back, Motley felt he was right up there with another Browns Hall of Famer. Jim Brown joined the Browns in 1957, and he went on to become one of the league's most celebrated running backs ever. Over nine seasons, all in Cleveland, Brown led the league in rushing yards eight times, rushing touchdowns five times, and rushing attempts six times. Motley, who never overlapped with Brown, was used differently in the offense.

"I didn't have the wide plays, the 'flip' like Jim had," Motley said, referring to what would be known in the modern era as the pitch. It's a play in which the quarterback "flipped" or "pitched" the ball back to the running back behind the line of scrimmage so the running back could get to the outside and use his speed for a big gain. "Paul (Brown) wouldn't give it to me," Motley said. "I asked him to flip the ball to me, and he said the play wasn't designed for me. What I did was go up the middle, trap plays, and straight away for short yardage."

Motley excelled at draws and the trap play, in which a defensive lineman was goaded into crossing the line of scrimmage only to become "trapped," creating an open space for the back to run through. People would complain that those were the only two plays that the Browns featured, but no one could stop them. "The trap was a fantastic play," Motley later said, "but I was seldom sent outside. There's no telling how much yardage I might have made if I ran as much as some backs do now."

Of course, as a fullback Motley was called upon to block, too.

While Motley's ability to run with the football was unrivaled at the time, he was also considered the best blocking back of his era. In fact, many of his teammates felt Motley's blocking skills were often overlooked. "He was the backbone of our passing attack," recalled Browns receiver Dante Lavelli, who remained close friends with Motley long after their playing days were over.

"The big thing I remember about Marion was his blocking and his quick acceleration for a big man. He was the first big man that could go from a standing start and burst through the middle and go 30, 40 yards and score a touchdown," Lavelli continued. "Many offenses are geared to the passing attack with a big fullback doing the blocking. But it's pretty hard to find one that has the spread and the shoulders that Marion had. I think he was around 44, 46 inches across there. He had the physical properties to be a good blocker. He realized that when he couldn't run the ball, he could do other things for the football team, and that was his outstanding blocking."

Don Shula, who would go on to become a Hall of Fame head coach, played with Motley in Cleveland in 1951 and 1952 and against him in 1953 and 1955. Shula once said of Motley, "He was a train wreck, and I was one of the guys he wrecked."

Browns teammate Lou Groza reminisced about a particular play that epitomized how hard Motley played. "We were playing Pittsburgh and (Motley) lost his helmet," Groza recalled. "About three different fellas had a shot at him, and he went and scored a touchdown, running down the field and bowling over people without a helmet on. That's the kind of spirit that Motley had in every ball game. He was just a fierce competitor."

Many opponents had similar stories about playing against

Motley and feeling his physical presence. Baltimore Colts Hall of Fame quarterback Johnny Unitas once said about Motley: "They don't keep stats for broken tackles, but if they did, Motley would be at the top of the list, because he routinely broke so many tackles and it was still hard to get the guy on the ground."

Then there was defensive end Charlie Powell, who became the youngest player in NFL history when he signed with the 49ers in 1952 at age 19. Powell, who played seven pro seasons with two teams, once said that when Motley ran the ball, it sounded like a rhinoceros coming through the line. Powell said he would hit Motley as low as he could, and if he tackled Motley, he would check his teeth and then get up. There was nothing like trying to tackle Motley with a full head of steam, he said.

In Motley's obituary years later for the *New York Times*, Otto Graham was quoted describing his former teammate as "the best fullback I ever saw, a better all-around player than Jimmy Brown." Before Blanton Collier took over as Browns head coach in 1963, he guided Motley as an assistant coach with Great Lakes and then the Browns. He went a step further in his praise, describing Motley as "the greatest all-around football player I ever saw."

Though Motley's stature these days has faded compared with Brown and other top running backs who came after, those who follow the game closely still recognize his impact. Decades later, at a 2021 press conference, Kansas City Chiefs coach Andy Reid was asked to compare a coming opponent, the physically dominant running back Derrick Henry, to another running back, past or present. Without hesitation, Reid replied, "Marion Motley. That was a good answer, wasn't it?"

Racism on the field was a constant for Marion Motley and other Black players.

CHAPTER 15

TACKLING RACISM

Marion Motley called it an "extracurricular activity:" the racism on the field that came with reintegrating professional football and breaking the sport's color barrier that had existed since 1933.

It became routine: The play would be over, then opposing players would stomp on Motley's hands and give their cleats a hard twist until his hands bled. Or they gave Motley a quick shot in the ribs while in a pile. Though Motley's teammates would come to his defense when they saw those things happen, they couldn't defend him all the time.

Motley and Bill Willis soon realized that they were going to hear racial slurs every game. Cheap shots from opponents were commonplace, too. And the referees were not going to be on the Black players' side. "When we first started, these (referees) would just stand right there and see those guys step on us and kick us and they would just turn their backs," Motley said.

The two players agreed that they couldn't lose their temper, because if they tried to get back at the opposing players, they risked being penalized or kicked off the team and losing this opportunity to play pro football. One time, Willis was so upset that he almost started a fight with an opposing player, but his teammates pulled him away from the altercation and told him they would take care of it on the next play.

Another time, when the Browns were playing the New York Yankees in the AAFC, Motley was trying to run with the ball when a defender jumped on his back to tackle him. Unable to bring Motley down, defender Harmon Rowe began slugging him in the face. Players didn't wear face masks at the time, so Motley just had to take it.

"Motley's whole style of play was so physically imposing, so for an opponent to have to punch him in the face while he's riding on his back shows how powerful he was, that they would go to any means to get him on the ground," Ohio sports historian Larry Phillips said. "The level of brutality that triggered that type of play tells us that he didn't get a lot of whistles, and they didn't throw the flag."

All of that physicality took a toll. After the Yankees game, Motley was being interviewed when a photographer asked him to smile. Motley said he couldn't because a few of his teeth got knocked out during the game.

Motley admitted that it was hard to not get back at his racist opponents. "We couldn't do anything," he said. "I'd just get up and want to kill 'em. But this is one of them things that Paul (Brown) told us when we first started. He said, 'You know, you two fellows are going to be into many scrapes and things of this type. People are (going) to be calling you names and things. You're going to have to stick it out.'"

In the 1988 book *Iron Men* by Stuart Leuthner, Motley said white players quickly learned what kind of players he and Willis were: "They found out that when they called us (the N-word), I was running for touchdowns and Bill was knocking the hell out of them."

***

The Browns traveled by airplane and bus to play games across the country. The South remained segregated, with Jim Crow laws still in effect. Because of this, Motley and Willis often had to stay in their hotel rooms the day before a game while their white teammates were out on the town. Or they would have to eat dinner alone in their rooms because they couldn't go into the same restaurants as their white teammates.

One of the more notable incidents came late in the 1946 season, when the Browns were still in the AAFC. With two games left on the schedule, Cleveland was set to travel to Miami to play the Seahawks. However, Brown was told that there had been death threats made against his two Black players. The threats went as far as to say that if Motley and Willis made the trip and stepped onto the field to play, they would be shot.

Brown took the threat seriously. He met with Motley and Willis before the team left for Miami and explained the situation. If the players wanted, he said, they could stay in Cleveland and miss the game but still be paid. The players accepted.

***

Motley said the Browns were a close-knit ballclub, and he credited that for why the organization won so many championships. Brown, at the top, set the standard.

There was another time in Miami when the coach was checking his team into a hotel before a game. The hotel manager said that "arrangements were made" for Motley and Willis to stay elsewhere. Brown would not have anything to do with such arrangements.

"Well, I guess that's fine," Brown told the hotel manager. "But you better know, if they go, we all go." The hotel manager thought for a moment and said, "Well, maybe we can set these guys up after all."

While Marion Motley, *front right*, was supported by his Browns teammates, he and his Black teammates endured constant abuse from opposing players.

This attitude helped the Browns' white players develop a level of respect and friendship with their Black teammates. Yet the reality was that Blacks coming up in America during the 1940s and 1950s had struggles throughout society—playing football, riding the bus, going shopping. If you were Black and you looked at a white person the wrong way—especially in the South—it could cost you your life.

Motley and Willis were strong physically, but when they hit the field and opposing players and fans called them names and used racial slurs, they had to be strong mentally. At times it was difficult for them to stay calm when those things were happening. Yet they did. They showed tremendous restraint. They rose above the hatred.

CHAPTER 16

SLOW PROGRESS FOR CHANGE

People laughed when Paul Brown's players showed up carrying notebooks ahead of the 1950 season. "As the years went by," Marion Motley said, "everyone had notebooks, even Green Bay." It was just one of many innovations that Brown brought to pro football.

Other Brown innovations later in his NFL career included using radio transmission headsets to communicate plays to his quarterback through his helmet (which is still used today), and an offensive blocking scheme known as "the cup." This strategy taught offensive linemen to block in the shape of a curve to protect the quarterback, which is an important blocking scheme that again is still used today. It was a big reason why Hall of Fame quarterback Otto Graham was such a prolific passer.

Brown was the first coach to determine that the 40-yard dash was an important measurement of speed for football players. Why? Because it was the best way to see how fast a player could reach a punt returner, who at the time was about 40 yards away.

And then there's the face mask. During a game in 1953, Graham took a hard hit to the face, opening up a deep gash.

Brown called on trainer Leo Murphy and equipment manager Morrie Kono to design something quickly that could be affixed to Graham's helmet to prevent or reduce any more facial injuries and allow the quarterback to stay in the game. The pair came up with an appliance to protect Graham's face, which became known as a face mask. Graham finished the second half, and the Browns won. Soon after, Brown made it mandatory that his players wear face masks, and other teams followed. The face mask largely became part of the NFL uniform by 1955. "Anything you can do to protect the players . . . it saved an awful lot of teeth and broken jaws. It progressed the game and made it better," Murphy said in a 2009 ESPN.com article.

Yet, the most significant of Brown's innovations was signing Black players.

***

College football has long been the gateway to pro football. During the 1940s and for several decades after, talented Black players tended to play at HBCUs because they were the only schools that offered an opportunity. Of course, the best programs—both in terms of athletics but also, in the eyes of many Americans, academics—were the mainstream institutions that still dominate today: think Michigan, Notre Dame, Ohio State, and Oklahoma.

For the Black players who might have gone on to play professionally after college, the prospect was a long shot before the 1933 "gentleman's agreement," and not on the table after that. And while baseball players at least had the Negro Leagues where the top Black stars could play their game, entertain crowds, and make a meager living, no such opportunities existed in pro football.

Motley and three others finally broke football's color line in 1946, yet the dam had hardly burst. At the start of the 1950s, most NFL teams still did not have Black players. As late as 1954, the league still had just 31 Black players.

Brown wasn't caught up in race. When building his rosters, he looked at a player's talent and character, not his skin color. This perspective goes back to his days growing up in Massillon, Ohio, playing with Black teammates in the early to mid-1920s, then returning after college to coach at his alma mater, Washington High School, where he had several Black players on his teams each year from 1932 to 1940. Once Brown took over his namesake team in Cleveland in 1946 and signed Bill Willis and Motley, Blacks in the community and across the country noticed: If a player was a good fit for his team, Brown was going to sign him.

Motley recalled that many of his teammates viewed Brown as "a cynical man." No one questioned his football acumen, though. "He could pick players," Motley said. "He made All-Americans and professional football players out of guys that you never heard of, and we turned out to be the best football players in the National Football League. He's a man that deserves the honor of being in the Hall of Fame."

***

The Browns and Rams began the process of righting a wrong when they signed Black players in 1946, reintegrating the sport after 12 years of segregation. Integration made sense at the box office, too. Even going back to the Browns' very first game in 1946, an estimated 10,000 Blacks came out to Cleveland Municipal Stadium to watch the 44–0 shellacking of the Miami Seahawks.

It's no doubt that having Motley and Willis on the team was a big reason for that.

"I have to believe that the owners took note of this as the turnstiles are turning a little bit faster," Bill Willis Jr. said. "Cleveland always had a big stadium, so not only did they have excellent players that could help them win, but they also saw the economic benefit as well."

With Motley, Willis, and later Horace Gillom on the roster, the Browns were beloved by the Black community in Cleveland. They also had the effect of giving Black youth heroes they could look up to. This trend continued a decade later when Jim Brown arrived as the team's next great Black star.

Breaking pro football's color line was just the first step, though. Fully reintegrating the sport took much longer. The racism and discrimination in pro football was deeply ingrained. Upending this required changes not just in pro football, but at lower levels, too.

While the door had opened on the pro game, many of the biggest universities remained predominantly white. Talented Black players had some opportunities to play at HBCUs, but the Atlantic Coast Conference didn't have its first Black player until 1963, and the Southwestern Conference waited three years longer. It took until 1967 for the SEC to have its first Black player. And those are just the first Black players. Some college teams didn't field a Black player until years later.

Nonetheless, according to former Pro Football Hall of Fame Executive Director Joe Horrigan, Black players who did find their way into the AAFC and NFL in the 1940s were coming from the white schools. It wasn't until the 1960s that HBCU players finally started receiving looks, and that wasn't from NFL teams. The upstart American Football League began play in 1960, hoping to challenge the established NFL, and in order to do this, its teams needed to find quality players to fill out their rosters. As a result, the AFL teams "began to tap into this untapped resource" of HBCUs, Horrigan said.

In a surprise to many, including those in the NFL, the AFL succeeded in its quest. The NFL agreed to let its champion face off with the winner of the AFL after the 1966 season in what's now known as Super Bowl I. An AFL team had beaten its NFL counterpart by Super Bowl III, and by the end of the decade the two leagues had merged. Historians can point to various reasons why the AFL succeeded where the AAFC did not, but the AFL's willingness to sign Black players, especially those from HBCUs, was a big one.

It took a while, but eventually Black colleges got their due by producing some of the greatest players pro football has ever seen. Among them were Chicago Bears running back Walter Payton (Jackson State) and San Francisco 49ers wide receiver Jerry Rice (Mississippi Valley State), both considered among the best of all time at their positions. In 1988 Washington Redskins quarterback Doug Williams (Grambling State) became the first Black quarterback to win a Super Bowl.

***

As shown most notably by Williams, just because Blacks had broken into pro football didn't mean they had fully broken into the lineups. Motley and Willis were elite at their positions, and they played for a coach in Brown who wasn't going to deny them playing there. Not everyone was so lucky. From the time the sport was reintegrated in 1946, the reality for most Black players was that they were only going to be permitted to play certain positions.

Black players were the victims of a trend called "stacking"— limiting Blacks mostly to positions that lined up on the outside of the field. Positions in the middle of the field, including quarterback and center on offense, and middle linebacker and safety on defense, were saved for the white athletes. "These were all positions where . . . most of the action occurred," Horrigan explained. "It was referred to as 'stacking' so-called smart, white players in the middle of the field. These positions were considered to be the thinking man's positions, and pro football owners felt that Black players weren't smart enough to play these positions."

As it went, the players in the middle of the field generally called the plays—the quarterback on offense, the center calling assignments for the rest of the offensive linemen, the middle linebacker making the calls on defense, and the safety making calls for the secondary. "It wasn't until 1969 that a Black quarterback started for his team, and a home opener for a season, and that was James Harris in Buffalo," said Horrigan, a Buffalo native. "But even after (Harris) was a starting quarterback, there just was slow growth at that position. Now, we don't even think about it. We no longer say a 'Black quarterback,' we just say a quarterback."

To illustrate just how long it's taken to get to that point, look no further than the case of Warren Moon. With a rifle for an arm, Moon started most of three seasons in college for Washington, and as a senior in 1977, he led the Huskies to the Rose Bowl. With three touchdowns—two rushing, one on a 28-yard pass—Moon earned MVP honors in a 27–20 win over Michigan.

Yet when it was time for the NFL Draft, word traveled to

Warren that he wasn't a top prospect. Not wanting to be left behind by the NFL, he instead signed with the Edmonton Eskimos of the Canadian Football League and became a star there, winning five Grey Cups as CFL champions in six seasons. Finally, in 1984, he got his chance in the NFL when the Houston Oilers signed him. Soon one of the league's prolific passers, Moon made nine Pro Bowls in 17 seasons. He became not only the first Black quarterback, but also the first undrafted quarterback, to be inducted into the Pro Football Hall of Fame.

While opportunities have grown for Black players on the field, barriers still exist. This is especially true on the sideline. Fritz Pollard, the NFL's first Black player, was also its first Black coach when he shared the Akron Pros' job with Elgie Tobin during the 1921 season. Pollard coached one more game, this time for the Hammond Pros, in 1925. After that? Nothing.

As more and more Black players began populating NFL rosters, the league noticed the coaching ranks remained mostly white. "In the '60s and even into the '70s, you could almost count the number of Black coaches around the league on one or two hands," Horrigan said. "It was that homogenous." In fact, there wasn't another Black head coach in the NFL for 64 years, when the maverick Al Davis hired his former offensive lineman Art Shell to be the head coach of his Los Angeles Raiders in 1989. It was the same year Shell was inducted into the Pro Football Hall of Fame. His arrival hardly opened the floodgates for other Black coaches, though.

Enter: the "Rooney Rule." Named for Pittsburgh Steelers owner Dan Rooney, the former chairman of the league's diversity committee, the 2003 initiative required teams to interview ethnic-minority candidates for head coaching and senior football operations positions. The rule was created so that NFL teams give qualified ethnic-minority candidates a fair and good-faith opportunity to interview for those positions.

Several prominent Black coaches were hired in the ensuing years. However, the lack of diversity on the sidelines persisted. After the 2021 season, the Miami Dolphins fired Brian Flores and the Houston Texans fired David Culley. That made Mike Tomlin of the Pittsburgh Steelers the lone Black head coach in the league. Although the Texans eventually hired a Black replacement in Lovie Smith, and Todd Bowles took over in Tampa Bay, that still left the league going into the 2022 season with just three Black head coaches—or 9 percent. According to a *Washington Post* analysis from that year, three other head coaches were also people of color. By comparison, nearly 60 percent of the league's players were Black, and 71 percent were people of color.

Shell's hiring had opened the door for Black head coaches, but the 2022 *Washington Post* analysis drove in just how few had been able to walk through. Among the 191 head coaches employed in the NFL over the 33 years after Shell was hired, only 25 of them were Black.

CHAPTER 17

FOOTBALL TRAILBLAZERS

"I look at some of the players today and wonder if they could've done what we did. Most of 'em, 99 percent, have no idea who I am."
— Marion Motley in a 1995 interview with the
Philadelphia Daily News.

In American history, Jackie Robinson has become a national hero—and for good reason. A former multi-sport star at UCLA, Robinson was toiling in baseball's Negro Leagues when Branch Rickey called. The Brooklyn Dodgers' president and general manager signed Robinson to a minor league contract to play the 1946 season in Montreal. The following year, on April 15, 1947, Robinson debuted for Brooklyn, breaking the color line in the country's most popular sport.

Facing racism at every step, Robinson proved mentally tough enough to battle on. Over his 10 seasons with the Dodgers, he became one of baseball's most dangerous hitters and most exciting base runners. And soon after his debut, other teams followed in signing Black players; before long America's pastime was reintegrated. As important as Robinson was, however, he wasn't the first to break the color line in U.S. pro team sports. While the wheels were turning in Brooklyn in 1946, the Los Angeles Rams signed Kenny Washington and Woody Strode. Then the Browns brought on Bill Willis and Marion Motley.

The pioneering football players are now talked about as a package deal—the four who broke pro football's color line together. Not all their careers were equal, though.

The dynamics in Los Angeles were a lot different than in Cleveland. In Cleveland, Paul Brown just wanted to win, and win with the best players. For him, race didn't matter. He made sure of that by emphasizing to his white players, and anyone around or involved with the organization, that he would not tolerate any racism towards Motley and Willis, or those racist players would be gone.

That wasn't the case for Washington and Strode in Los Angeles. Rams owner Dan Reeves had integrated his team only because he had to in order to secure a stadium. And he wasn't counting on Washington and Strode to be integral members of the team's success. He just wanted to quiet critics like Halley Harding, the former Negro Leagues player and *Los Angeles Tribune* writer who had been leading the movement to force the Rams to integrate.

Washington, a running back, was already 27 when he signed with the Rams and 28 by the time the season started. After UCLA, he had played for the Hollywood Bears in the Pacific Coast Professional Football League and done a stint as a sports ambassador with the USO during World War II, visiting troops and playing in exhibition games. Though Washington had been an all-league player with the Bears, he came to the Rams with bad knees from five surgeries and many years of wear and tear playing the game.

Strode was even older, with his 32nd birthday coming during training camp. An end (wide receiver in today's game), he had also been playing for the Hollywood Bears when World War II broke out. Strode joined the US Army Air Corps, where he unloaded bombs in Guam and the Mariana Islands. After the war, Strode was working for the Los Angeles County district attorney's office serving subpoenas and escorting prisoners when he got the call to join the Rams. By then, though, Strode's best days had already fleeted.

Woody Strode, *front right*, and Kenny Washington, *back left*, pose with Los Angeles Rams teammates ahead of the 1946 season. Though stars in college, both were past their primes by the time they got an opportunity in the pros.

"Both players were past their prime when they were signed with the Rams," *USA Today* NFL columnist Jarrett Bell said. "When they got an opportunity to play, the conditions under which they played in Los Angeles were just horrendous to hear about. The owner didn't really care whether they got along with the rest of the team or not. It was just something that they were mandated to do because they were given permission to play in the Coliseum."

Washington and Strode's experiences in Los Angeles were so bad that Strode once said in a *Sports Illustrated* article, "Integrating the NFL was the low point in my life. If I have to integrate heaven, I don't want to go." And for what? In 1971, Strode was quoted as saying, "History doesn't know who we are." As *Los Angeles Times* opinion writer Matthew Fleischer pointed out in a 2019 op-ed, the statement was "as true now as when he said it."

Bell added: "I think the travesty with Washington and Strode was the fact that they weren't really able to come into the NFL in the prime of their careers, unlike Motley and Willis, where they had long sustained careers and became Hall of Famers. But Washington and Strode did help open the door, no doubt about that. Their place in history is revered still to this day, even though you wonder if a lot of the players of today have even heard of them."

Mike Brown, Paul Brown's son, said his dad would have been unaware of what was going on in Los Angeles at the time. "I remember him saying to me that he wasn't trying to create some new policy for the country," Mike Brown said. "My dad said he was trying to make his team in Cleveland better. He felt they (Motley and Willis) were the best players and that they would make his team better, so they deserved a chance. . . . I don't think in his mind he was trying to do anything beyond that."

That was a fact substantiated in Paul Brown's autobiography, *PB: The Paul Brown Story,* when he wrote, "I never considered football players black or white, nor did I keep or cut a player just because of his color."

That's not to say that Motley and Willis were free from intense scrutiny and pressure in Cleveland. They both understood that and took it upon themselves to carry that weight, not only for themselves, but for any other Black players who would possibly come after them. "Willis and I pioneered this whole thing for the young Negroes today because if Willis and I had been anywhere near a hothead . . . it would have been another 10 years," Motley said in an interview during a Hall of Fame luncheon. "We would have set them back another 10 years, 15 years to get a chance."

***

Motley and Willis never disregarded or diminished the history Washington and Strode made when they reintegrated the NFL. Motley acknowledged exactly what those men went through and shared the same brutal experiences—both physical and mental. The difference was that Washington and Strode were set up to fail from the start. Washington had a decent three-year NFL career, with his best season coming in 1947 when he averaged 7.4 yards per carry. Strode played for the Rams for just one season, in 1946, and saw action in 10 games, catching four passes for a total of 37 yards.

"Strode and Washington, I think, were political pawns at that time," Ohio sports historian Larry Phillips said. "I hope that doesn't sound harsh, but I think that's what they were. History kind of lends itself to that kind of supposition. But obviously Motley and Willis were not. They were Hall of Fame players, clearly elite national talents that people had problems dealing with in the NFL for years."

Not everyone in the NFL shared Paul Brown's conviction in equal opportunity. "He knew that there were people in the league that wouldn't approve it, and it didn't bother him one iota," Mike Brown said. "He did what he felt was right."

The "people" Mike Brown is talking about were led by one powerful man: Redskins owner George Preston Marshall. Openly racist, Marshall was famously determined to keep the Redskins all white, and they stayed that way long after the other NFL teams integrated. He finally integrated the team only because he had to. With the Redskins' stadium—later and best known as RFK Memorial Stadium—being on federal land, the government threatened to revoke the team's 30-year lease unless Marshall signed a Black player.

The team finally did so in 1962. In that year's NFL Draft, the Redskins selected Heisman Trophy winner Ernie Davis, a Black running back from Syracuse, but traded him to Cleveland for flanker Bobby Mitchell, who then became the first Black player signed by Marshall. "I am surprised that with the world on the brink of another war they are worried about whether or not a Negro is going to play for the Redskins," Marshall said in an interview at the time.

Bell described Marshall as being "the linchpin, if you will, for excluding Blacks from the NFL." And Marshall wasn't exactly enthusiastic about Paul Brown singing Motley and Willis.

"But it never bothered my dad one bit," Mike Brown said.

"It's best to remember the country . . . you had southerners, and they were ingrained with an attitude towards Blacks. That didn't make them bad people. That was how they were brought up to understand the world. And we were up here in northeastern Ohio, where it was different. We didn't believe in all this stuff they were doing in the South. We thought it was wrong, and my dad was raised in Northeast Ohio, and that was his attitude. That's how I was raised, and it's a part of my life that I've always been proud of."

CHAPTER 18

OPENING DOORS

As a star two-way player for Penn State, Dave Robinson became the school's first Black player to earn All-America honors when he did so in 1962. Then, as a linebacker, he played 12 seasons in the NFL, where he helped the Green Bay Packers win Super Bowls I and II. He's now enshrined in both the College Football Hall of Fame and the Pro Football Hall of Fame. Several Black athletes inspired his career, Robinson said, but three in particular stood out.

"When you started talking about athletes, in our household there were only three athletes in the world to talk about: Jackie Robinson, Joe Louis, and Marion Motley," said Robinson, who grew up in New Jersey. "I eventually met Jackie Robinson and Joe Louis later in my life, but when I met Marion Motley, I knew I had come full circle."

After his playing days, Robinson lived in Ohio for a time, moved away, then moved back in 1979. That's when he met the man he came to revere. "Motley was one of the first guys I met when I moved back to Ohio, and I instantly fell in love with the guy," Robinson said. "He was a great, sweet gentleman. He was one of my idols growing up."

Among the many things that Robinson admired about Motley was his genuine kindness. "Motley was a big influence in my life," Robinson said. "I can't think of anyone who met Marion Motley who didn't like him. He aged well. He didn't have arguments with people. He didn't hold any grudges about what he went through, and what we went through in those times. I would walk through fire for him. He was a great person, a superman among men. He was someone I wanted to emulate in my older years."

Seventeen years after Marion Motley debuted with the Cleveland Browns, Dave Robinson began his Hall of Fame career with the Green Bay Packers. A linebacker, Robinson played the first 10 of his 12 NFL seasons in Green Bay, starting in 1963.

To understand Robinson's adulation for Motley, it helps to understand the similarities between the two men and what they encountered during their football careers. In 1961, Robinson became the first Black player to take part in the Gator Bowl in Jacksonville, Florida, where Penn State beat Georgia Tech. After leading the Nittany Lions to a 9–1 record in 1962, he and the team returned to Jacksonville, this time to play Florida. His experiences in the state had parallels to what Motley and Willis endured during the 1940s and 1950s.

When they arrived in late December 1962, the Penn State players went for a meal at the Orlando airport, only to have Robinson turned away. His teammates, in solidarity, walked out with him. Soon after, in Jacksonville, they found their counterparts from Florida wearing Confederate flag decals on their helmets. Racism and segregation were openly displayed throughout the South—sunny Florida included.

During the week Penn State was preparing for the Gator Bowl, Robinson received mail that was withheld from him until after the game. When he finally received the mail, he described it as being an inch thick, stacked together.

"It was unbelievable, because 99 percent of the letters were talking about how they were gonna kill me if I played in the game," Robinson said. "The one I remember most was the guy who said he was an army veteran classified expert with a rifle, and that he was gonna take his gun to the Gator Bowl, and when they introduced me and I came out on the field he was going to shoot me on the 50-yard line on national TV. Well, he actually said, 'When that bear comes on the field, I'm gonna shoot him.'"

Robinson said he wasn't as concerned about the death threat as much as he was being called a bear. "That made me mad because I hate bears," Robinson said, his voiced filled with befuddlement, then laughter. "Why did he call me a bear? That's what got me mad. He called me a bear, man."

Florida, though coming in as the underdog with a 6–4 record, ended up winning the game 17–7. An MVP was named for each team; Robinson took the honors for Penn State.

NFL teams didn't actively scout Black players at the time, Robinson later recalled, but a recommendation from Penn State coach Joe Paterno was enough to convince Vince Lombardi. The legendary Green Bay Packers coach, for whom the Super Bowl trophy is now named, picked Robinson in the first round. Upon signing with Green Bay, Robinson looked at the team's roster and began to regret his decision.

"I saw a quarterback from Alabama. One running back from LSU. The other running back was from Louisville, Kentucky. Half the defense and offensive line was from Texas," he told the Athletic in 2021. "Every time I had gone south of the Mason-Dixon Line, I had not had a very good experience the few times we played down there. I was like, 'What have I done?'"

It turned out discrimination wouldn't be a problem in Green Bay—at least not within the team. Robinson said Lombardi, who had experienced discrimination as an Italian American growing up in New York, simply didn't allow it within his team. Like Paul Brown in the 1940s, Lombardi refused to let race be a factor.

That showed in his actions. In 1961, Lombardi drafted Black defensive back Herb Adderley in the first round, then picked Robinson two years later. Robinson said Lombardi was being pressured by management not to draft Black players. "The board of directors came to Vinny and said, 'We're not trying to tell you what to do, but you're wasting draft choices. You don't have to pick a Black guy until the third round.' Vince said, 'We don't draft by color in Green Bay, we draft by football ability. You guys handle the finances, and I'll handle the team. The only colors we have in Green Bay are green and gold,' and they said, 'Yes, sir.'"

Lombardi also tried to take care of discrimination against his players around Green Bay. Robinson recalled that there were a handful of bars and restaurants in Green Bay that would not allow Blacks in the 1960s. Like Brown, Lombardi wanted his Black players to have the same access as the white players.

"Vince called all the owners to his office, and Vince reportedly said, 'You guys work and own your buildings, and you can deny service to anybody you don't want to see. In fact, I'll even go to war to protect your right to deny service. But if you guys don't want the African American Packers in your bars and restaurants, they won't be there as of this day. In fact, I'll tell you this, neither will the white Packers. So, you guys are off limits to all my players."

After that, Robinson said, there were no more places where the Black players couldn't go to eat in Green Bay.

CHAPTER 19

END OF THE LINE

The beginning of the end of Marion Motley's playing career took place at that 1951 College All-Star Game when Paul Brown made him play through a knee injury. The residual of the preseason injury was apparent. Motley played in 11 games during the 1951 season and carried the ball just 61 times for 273 yards, his lowest total by far in his six seasons with the Browns to that point. Cleveland still reached the NFL Championship Game but lost 24–17 to the Los Angeles Rams. Motley started and carried the ball five times for 23 yards. He also had one reception for 23 yards.

Motley stuck around after that, but he was no longer the player he once was. In 1952, Motley was serviceable, gaining 444 yards on 104 carries in 12 games with just one touchdown. The Browns reached the NFL Championship Game once again, but this time they lost to the Detroit Lions 17–7, with Motley coming off the bench to carry the ball six times for 74 yards. He also had three receptions for 21 yards. The next season, the Browns played in their fourth consecutive NFL Championship Game, losing to the Lions once again, this time 17–16. Motley played in the game but did not start and had no carries. That followed a 1953 season in which Motley, now 33 years old, played in 12 games and carried the ball just 32 times for 161 yards. He did not score a touchdown all year. It was his lowest output in his eight-year Browns career. His bad knees were the culprit.

The 1953 season was Motley's last with the Browns. That offseason, he received some surprising news. "Coach Paul Brown just came to me one day and said, 'You are retired.' Then I read it in the papers. So, I retired," Motley recalled in an interview with the *Pittsburgh Post-Gazette* on September 22, 1955.

Motley sat out the 1954 season due to his involuntary retirement. He wasn't quite ready to give it up yet, though. Before the 1955 season, Motley, at 35, decided he wanted to unretire. That was easier said than done. The Browns still owned his rights, and they didn't think he could be productive for them. Believing Motley to be past his prime, they traded him to the Pittsburgh Steelers for fullback Ed Modzelewski. Brown did not tell Motley he was traded.

"The way it was done, it left a bad taste in my mouth," Motley later said in a United Press International article from March 31, 1976. "Paul Brown was the greatest coach I ever saw, and I liked him. He taught me about life, but I felt he could've handled my trade to Pittsburgh a little different."

Pittsburgh brought Motley in with the intention of playing him as a linebacker. Seeing the field sparingly during that 1955 season, most of his action ended up coming on special teams. Rushing the ball just twice—once in the opener, then again in Week 2—Motley accumulated eight yards. On October 31, after appearing in six games, the Steelers released him. That's when Motley retired officially, at age 35.

"Well, my knees were still a big factor," he said later. "They ached and they hurt. It was becoming a job. When this game of football becomes a job, you better quit it."

The news of Motley's release received little fanfare.

The Cleveland *Plain Dealer*'s Chuck Heaton later interviewed Motley for a 1968 article. They discussed his career and, among other things, the disparity in pay between players in Motley's era and those currently playing. Motley's top salary for a season never exceeded $12,000, which is about $130,000 in 2022 dollars. While that wage was hardly a pittance—the average American family in 1950 earned $3,300, according to the U.S. Census Bureau—it hardly compares to the salaries players earned just a few decades later, much less today.

"As far as salary is concerned, I guess I just came along too early," Motley told Heaton. "I'm not complaining, though. Football gave me my start and I've kept going from there. I've been able to keep some property I bought while I was a player and I've kept moving ahead."

***

Ohio sports historian Larry Phillips presented a novel concept for contextualizing the greatness of Motley's career. Consider, he said, an all-time draft of Ohio players. "And think about who's played football in Ohio," Phillips said, name-dropping some of the sport's all-time greats.

There's Benny Friedman, the great tailback from the 1920s and 1930s who was born and raised in Cleveland. Or Pete Henry of Mansfield, a tackle who played around the same time. Later, in the Super Bowl era, Alliance native Len Dawson led the Kansas City Chiefs to victory in Super Bowl IV, while fellow quarterback and Cincinnati native Roger Staubach led the Dallas Cowboys to two Super Bowl wins in the 1970s. Each of those guys is now in the Hall of Fame. More recently, Ben Roethlisberger of Findlay won two rings with the Steelers. He retired in 2021, the same year that Joe Burrow, of the small town of The Plains, led the Cincinnati Bengals to the Super Bowl in just his second pro season. Ohio has also produced the likes of Hall of Famers Cris Carter, Larry Csonka, Jack Lambert, Orlando Pace, Alan Page, Paul Warfield, and Charles Woodson, to name a few more.

For Phillips, the first pick in such a draft comes down to three names.

"It would be either Roger Staubach, Marion Motley, or Pete Henry," he said. "It depends on how you want to build your team."

Phillips explained that if you wanted to build your team with a franchise quarterback, then he would take Staubach over Dawson. Both have a strong case: Staubach played 11 seasons in Dallas, winning 85 games and earning MVP honors in Super Bowl VI after the 1971 season. Dawson played 19 pro seasons, won 94 games, and was the MVP of Super Bowl IV after the 1969 season. If you wanted to build your team around line play, Phillips's pick would be Henry, because he was a two-way lineman who could protect the quarterback at his offensive tackle position and could effectively rush the opposing quarterback on the defensive line.

"But if you want to build your team around an all-time running back, who can run, who can block, who had tremendous size and incredible versatility, it has to be Marion Motley," Phillips said. "And Paul Brown did build a franchise around him."

Many others have shared similar praise. During a radio interview, Otto Graham once said: "I know there were a lot of great football players throughout the history of the game, a lot of great fullbacks, but in my opinion, Marion Motley is the best fullback who ever played football." Paul Brown went a step further, saying Motley would've been a Hall of Fame linebacker if that was the only position he played.

***

At a banquet in Motley's honor just before he was inducted into the Hall of Fame, Brown gave an impassioned speech about his former player. "Marion Motley was a combination of size and speed beyond any man I ever had," Brown said. "He was a tremendous physical specimen. As you know. Marion was much more than just a ball carrier . . . he went way beyond just being a great ball carrier. He was one of the reasons that Otto was as great as he was. Marion's blocking was tremendous, and as a defensive linebacker, probably as good a one as we ever had, but he played on the offense, he was a very rounded football player.

"But over and beyond all that was the fact that he had the interest of his team," Brown continued. "He was not a selfish football player. He was in the spirit of his club. He never knew, I don't think, how many yards he made in a given day. He was tremendously popular with his teammates. They liked him. I think maybe the fact that we won so many times attests to the importance of this kind of a man on your football team. I would have to say to you that he is the greatest back I had ever had."

In return, Motley said, "We had some good and bad times too, but to me, here's a coach that undoubtedly was the greatest coach that I had been under."

CHAPTER 20

MARION MOTLEY VS. ART MODELL

For as much as Marion Motley gave to the Cleveland Browns, for as much as he tolerated for the Cleveland Browns, all he wanted in return after his playing days were over was the opportunity to coach for the team he loved. The Browns never gave him that chance. Why not? Motley never got an answer. Was it race? Of course it was, he later surmised. With his playing career over, Motley felt he had the intellectual skills and knowledge of the game to transition into a quality coach. The owner of the Browns at the time, Art Modell, became Motley's public enemy No. 1 when he wouldn't give the former star a chance to coach—citing many feeble excuses, as far as Motley was concerned.

Motley's experience with Modell seemed to be a precursor to the feelings that most Browns fans would have toward this man who ripped their hearts out decades later. It stems from 1995, when Modell, through what some media outlets reported as "secret negotiations," announced he was moving the beloved Browns to Baltimore after the '95 season. (The NFL, knowing Cleveland boasted one of the most loyal fan bases in the league, committed to installing a new Cleveland expansion franchise starting with the 1999 season.)

That anger and contempt fans felt in 1995 mirrored how Motley and Browns fans felt about the owner in the early 1960s. In 1963, Modell had owned the team for two years when the team's former star fullback asked for a coaching position. Turning him down was not Modell's first highly unpopular decision that year. In January, Modell stunned the NFL community when he fired the coach his team was named for, Paul Brown. Just how well did that go over? A 2013 *Columbus Dispatch* article was headlined: "Paul Brown's dismissal stings 50 years later." The decision wasn't any more popular in 1963.

By then Motley had been retired from the NFL for nearly a decade, and during that time, he could not find any coaching positions in professional football. He saw many of his former teammates such as Otto Graham land coaching positions throughout the league, but Motley never could. He later spoke at length about his efforts to work with Modell.

"I asked Art Modell if I could scout Negro schools and help in the signing of Negro players," Motley recalled. "Modell called in (Browns head coach) Blanton Collier, and the three of us discussed it. Each of them thought this was a very good idea. Then when football season came, I waited for about half of the football season to hear from them." The call never came. Motley went to former teammate Dante Lavelli, who was scouting for the Browns at the time, seeking answers.

"I called Lavelli and asked him, 'What the hell is going on up there? Nobody has called me or anything?'" Motley said. "He said, 'Well, I don't know, Marion.' So, I said, 'I'll tell you what, if they don't call me in soon and send me out, I'm going to call a newspaper.'"

Motley waited more than half the season for an assignment. "It never came," Motley continued. "One day I went to the office and asked (Browns director of player personnel) Paul Bixler when was I to go out to a scouting assignment? He referred me to Art Modell. I had to catch Art in football practice to ask him about the scouting. He's kneeling on one knee looking at practice. He doesn't look around and give me no considerations or even turn around to look at me. He looks out on the football field, and he tells me, 'Well, Motley, you know what: the only thing you can help us doing is sign ballplayers.' And I said, 'Is that what you think?' And he said, 'Yeah. That's about the only thing I think you can help us on.' And I said, 'Well, I thank you,' and turned around and walked off the field."

In Motley's eyes, the owner's response meant only one thing. "This led me to believe that he had doubt as to whether I had the knowledge and qualification of knowing a (professional) football player," Motley said. Soon after that encounter, Motley said the Browns called and wanted him to go to Wilberforce College, a historically Black college just outside of Dayton, to scout the team. "Wilberforce had nothing. Neither one of the two ballclubs had anybody (to sign)," Motley said. "It was mainly them just doing this as an appeasement to keep me from saying anything." Realizing that Modell had no intention of hiring Motley to coach, Motley decided to write an open letter about the situation and took that letter to the *Pittsburgh Courier*, once the country's most widely circulated Black newspaper with a national circulation of almost

200,000. The paper, behind sports editor Bill Nunn Jr., ran the letter in its entirety on February 20, 1965.

Motley's letter ran more than 1,000 words, painstakingly documenting his version of the events. "Is the city of Cleveland, the so-called best location in the nation, the city, which is proud of its great record of equal opportunity in sports, afraid to take one more giant step forward?" the letter began.

As the letter continued, Motley said he "cannot remain silent" after hearing the news that the Browns signed a new assistant from outside the organization.

"About one year ago, I inquired at the Brown's (sic) offices about a coaching job or some sort of affiliation in any meaningful capacity," he continued. "At this time, I was told that there were no vacancies on the coaching staff. After hearing of the hiring of the new assistant, I now wonder if the full staff was the real reason or if the real reason is whether or not the time is right to hire a Negro coach in Cleveland on the professional level."

Motley continued on, describing his faith that Paul Brown would help him. "But in return for the respect, loyalty, and all out performance for this man that I had given in every game, his only reply was, 'Have you tried the Steel Mill?'"

Reminding readers of his long history with the Browns and specifically with Brown, going back to the Navy days, Motley wrote, "I have had many friends, both white and Negro, who have asked me why I am not affiliated with the Browns' organization. It has long been an established fact that most great athletes of one organization or another have been placed back in the organization upon retiring. This again brings me to my question. . . . Is the time ripe for the hiring of a Negro in the city of Cleveland in professional sports?"

Motley then shared the story of Modell asking him to scout Black colleges, but how he "sat around over a half of the season waiting for them to give me an assignment, it never came."

In conclusion, Motley wrote: "In writing this, I am not begging or asking for charity but like Jim Brown, I, too, have 'something to get off my chest.' I hope this will not lead to the hiring of me or any other Negro without thought being given to qualification and knowledge of the particular sport because I am not writing this for sympathy but only for the hiring of whomever it may be for their knowledge and not their color."

Soon after the letter was printed, Motley and Modell had a confrontation at a Browns practice. Motley had accused Modell of questioning his intelligence when it came to understanding the game at an executive level. "He (Modell) said, 'I don't think you wrote that letter.' I said, 'Oh, you calling me a dummy?' He said, 'Oh no, no, no. I didn't call you that. I just know . . . ' 'Yeah, you just told me I'm a dummy. This is what you feel all the way along. You think that I'm a dummy. When I asked you for a scouting job, you thought I couldn't do it. You tell me, the only thing I can help you do (is sign) ballplayers. Otherwise, you are telling me I'm a dummy.'"

One word led to another, Motley recalled, and Modell was "red in the face and blew his top." Then, Motley said, "I stood there and looked at him and laughed at him and walked on away. He's a prejudiced son of a bitch. I don't mind telling him, either. The guy is not right."

While vacationing in Palm Springs, California, Modell defended his actions, telling an Associated Press reporter that "Motley has done some scouting of players for us. And we hope to continue to use him in that capacity. He never asked me about coaching." Modell said he considered Motley "a legendary figure in pro football. He has a tremendous record as a player, and he also is a wonderful man."

Around the time Modell was telling Motley there were no significant coaching positions available, the Browns had hired Bob Nussbaumer as an end coach and assistant in the personnel department. In the AP interview, Modell defended that decision. "Nussbaumer was hired because his background and experience fitted him to handle specific jobs," Modell said. "My position on Negroes needs no defense, nor does the record of the Browns over the years," Modell added. "We are represented by scouts at every major Negro school."

That was it for Motley. After that confrontation on the field and in the media with Modell, Motley knew there was never going to be an opportunity to coach for the Cleveland Browns, or in the NFL for that matter. What mattered to Motley, though, was that he showed his integrity in facing Modell and telling the owner exactly how he felt, even though he knew a potential NFL coaching career was gone forever.

"Marion always tried to help people," recalled Dave Robinson, the Hall of Fame Black linebacker who experienced racism when he played during the 1960s and 1970s. "And the one thing that bothered him the most was that he always felt and thought he'd be an excellent assistant coach for the Browns, but he never got that opportunity, and that hurt him because that's the one thing he wanted to accomplish in life. The truth is, Marion had the personality that could charm a room. He had the type of personality players would have gravitated to. He tried, bless his heart, but he never got that opportunity."

With that door shut, Motley tried finding a meaningful career in other industries through which he could support his family, which by then included sons Ronald, Raymond, and Phillip (Motley and Eula Coleman divorced in 1962), as well as a son George, who had a different mother. It wasn't easy.

Motley said he had made up his mind that he wouldn't go broke after football like other players he'd heard about, no matter what he had to do. Some of his jobs included working as a dump truck driver, a mail carrier delivering packages, and an employee for a whiskey distributor. He worked for a county tax department and the Ohio Lottery. He also owned a bar and even tried to start a home remodeling business that failed.

"There was no money. I wasn't making any money," Motley said. "So, I just took anything. I'd work anywhere as long as I could make it. I dropped from something like $250 a week to, when I worked for the county, I made 62 dollars and 50 cents a week. It was a somewhat of a letdown."

The only notable head coaching job Motley ever acquired was in 1967 when Cleveland theatrical agent Sid Friedman hired him to coach the USA Daredevils, who are considered the first professional women's tackle football team in history. The Cleveland-based team eventually played other women's teams from Detroit, Pittsburgh, and Toronto, with Motley coaching until their league folded in 1973.

Veteran NFL Network analyst Steve Wyche said the way

Motley and other former great Black athletes were treated after their careers was a sad commentary on society. It harkened back to an earlier generation when Jesse Owens, fresh off winning four gold medals at the 1936 Summer Olympics, was relegated to racing against horses. No matter how great the Black athlete had been in his career, job opportunities later in life were scarce. "People said it was degrading for an Olympic champion to run against a horse," Owens once said. "But what was I supposed to do? I had four gold medals, but you can't eat four gold medals."

Wyche said he hoped Motley's legacy could be a teaching moment. "I think it's important to know what he accomplished for a lot of African Americans and for what they did or tried to do, whether on or off the football field," Wyche said. "If you don't know your history, if you don't know your past, it's going to be hard to live in your present and your future because they set the table.

"I mean this guy was a hero, and you saw all of the things he did on the football field," Wyche continued. "This is a Pro Football Hall of Famer who, when called upon the field of duty, he did it. Yet, when he called favors for the people who called favors on him when he was a football player, he was turned down. 'Can I get a job as a coach?' 'Uh, sorry Marion . . . we don't have a spot to fill.' 'Hey, can I get a job as a coach with your team?' 'Nah, you really don't fit.' Marion's story is a story of perseverance and denial that a lot of people (of color) still face today, and these are things that people have to understand have happened for a long time, and until we change, certain things are going to continue."

CHAPTER 21

AN EVERYDAY HERO

Marion Motley reached the pinnacle in his sport with his induction into the Pro Football Hall of Fame—and in his hometown no less—in 1968. To many Cantonians, Motley was bigger than life, and they were proud to call him one of their own. Yet, Motley shied away from the praise, almost not wanting the attention to be on him.

"Marion became such a community icon. . . . This is hard to believe, but he became so familiar with everybody that they tended to forget who he was in a sense," said Joe Horrigan, the former Pro Football Hall of Fame executive director. "He just became a member of the community, just another guy. That's how he wanted to be treated, and it was how he was treated." Horrigan said Motley would pick up his fan mail on Saturdays at the Hall of Fame. "And anytime we asked him, 'Hey Marion, there's a high school team here touring the building, would you mind meeting them and saying a few words to them?' Marion would say, 'No problem!' There were no airs about him. That was the beauty of Marion Motley."

Motley had been away from the game for 13 years by the time he was inducted. By then he just wanted to be a regular person. And to certain people, he was just that.

"He never was standoffish and didn't see himself as bigger or better than anybody else," retired Pro Football Hall of Fame President and Executive Director Stephen Perry said. "He loved to tell jokes, life-of-the-party type of guy. I loved being around him and was surprised that he was so down-to-earth."

To his family, Motley was that and more. "My grandfather was one of those old-school guys who would just have a conversation with you no matter who you were," grandson Tony Motley said. "He had so much insight on so many different things."

Another grandson, Joe Dose, echoed those sentiments. "To me he was just Grandpa," Dose said, "but when he came to my football games, or my basketball games when I was young, the fathers of my friends would be in awe of him, while I was thinking, 'That's just my grandpa.' I didn't know or understand what he had accomplished, what he had done in his career and his life until I got older."

Dose said his best memories of his grandfather were when Motley would take him to the parades and induction ceremonies at the Hall of Fame as a kid. "We'd be going different places to dinners and parades, and the induction ceremonies themselves," Dose said, "and I would say, 'Grandpa, when do we need to be there? When do you need to be at the parade?' He would say, 'Whenever we get there.' He was so laid-back, so . . . chill. He did things at his own pace."

At the same time, Dose, as an adult looking back, would often analyze how and why his grandpa could be so "laid-back" and "chill," knowing what he had gone through—the racism on and off the field, and the hatred towards him because he was Black. Dose always wondered how his grandpa didn't just . . . let loose.

"A lot in my mind goes back to his upbringing with his family. He was a southern gentleman," Dose continued. "He was raised to be respectful and obedient from his father. I remember talking to him about it. I would ask him, 'Grandpa, how did you put up with that?' His response was that if he wanted to play (professional football), if he acted out and gave anyone any reason to get rid of him or put him on the side, then it would be bad for all Black people. He told me that in order to play, he needed to hold his composure. He would tell me, 'If I was stepped on during one play, I would get my revenge on the very next play and do it the right way by running them over.'"

Joe's dad, Raymond Motley, was Marion and Eula's middle son. Raymond had been helping Marion coach the women's football team, the USA Daredevils, when he fell for Betty Dose, the team's quarterback. Joe grew up in Madison, Ohio, about an hour east of Cleveland, right off Lake Erie. The son of a Black dad and white mom, Joe said being biracial has "often been part of my struggle through life, about where I fit in." He was one of only six Black kids in his high school. "I would walk down the hall and get spit on, and I'm like, 'What in the hell?' and I would be ready to throw some fists," he said, looking back with embarrassment. "But what does that do? I'm a Black kid. I'm going to get kicked out of school. I'm going to get the worst punishment, right? I was like, 'No! I'm here to get an education and go to college.' My grandpa instilled in me, 'Don't let them know that they got to you because you have the power of response. When they know they bother you or hurt you, that's when they win, so don't let them get that victory.' That's why it's definitely in the back of my mind, even now, the restraint, and patience, and maintaining the power of response. You can only control your reaction." Dose graduated in 1999 from Bowling Green State University, the same place where his grandpa used to participate in training camp for the Browns, with a bachelor's degree in communications and marketing.

***

After their playing careers, Motley and Bill Willis remained close. "They developed a really strong bond and friendship," Dose recalled, adding, "A lot of it was based on the trials and tribulations they went through together. They were able to confide in each other. They loved and respected each other."

Willis's son, Bill Willis Jr., shared similar stories. "They were both loved and well respected by their teammates," Willis Jr. said. "I mean, I've seen photos and video footage of Browns outings, which Paul Brown was famous for, and he was always bringing the players and their families together to interact as a family. They were all very much a family. They looked out for each other. They cared for each other, and they cared for their fellow teammates as human beings."

Later in life, Willis Jr. recalled meeting Motley. "I don't know his exact dimensions, but to me as a kid, Marion Motley was the biggest Black man I had ever seen," he said. "I mean, he was thick, and he was large. He had two large kids, and I believe he had a Great Dane. I mean everything about him was large, but he was as gentle as the day is long."

While Motley and Willis are forever connected, Horace Gillom was a close contemporary. After playing for Brown at Massillon Washington High School and Ohio State, then following Motley to Nevada, he joined Motley and Willis on the Browns in 1947, becoming the team's third Black player.

Keith Herring, Gillom's nephew, knew of his uncle's athletic exploits as a professional player from the stories his family told him. Herring also got to know more about Motley personally through the Pro Football Hall of Fame festivities that take place every year in Canton. A longtime volunteer for the Hall, Herring would drive the Hall of Fame players, past and present, wherever they needed to be. For several years, Herring served as Motley's personal driver.

"I'm really proud that I had the opportunity to meet Mr. Motley, and that my son got a chance to meet him," Herring said. "My son was a running back, and Mr. Motley gave him a few pointers, and you know, sitting there watching that, I wish I could've had a camera recording Marion Motley giving my son some tips on running the ball and how to be a good football player. It was an honor to get to meet Mr. Motley and drive him around."

***

You couldn't talk about Motley without mentioning how much he loved smoking cigars and playing golf, according to fellow Hall of Famer Dave Robinson. One of Motley's friends who worked at the Hall of Fame, Dave Motts, concurred. After Motley's football playing days were over, he would stop into the Hall of Fame three or four times a month on Saturdays to pick up his mail. "Marion led with his cigar," Motts said.

Robinson said you could smell the cigar smoke when you got into Motley's car and after you got out. "That was the only bad thing he did," Robinson said, laughing sheepishly, as if he were telling on a classmate. Robinson said Motley didn't pinch pennies, either. "He loved good cigars, not those cheap, 10-cent cigars," he said. "I remember the first time I took a trip to the Caribbean islands; I made it a point to get a Cuban cigar and smuggle it back for Marion. The look on his face when he got it was worth a million dollars."

Robinson told a story about taking a trip back to State College, where he was an All-American for Penn State, to play in a golf outing. "Marion put the cigar in his mouth, and we'd be riding down the road and I could see the ash getting longer and longer, and I'd be thinking, 'He's going to drop that ash in my car.' He'd always wake up when that ash got an inch long, tap it into the ashtray, and would fall asleep again."

Robinson also had many memories with Motley on the golf course. Motley had diabetes, Robinson said, and one day they were on hole No. 7 when Motley had a request: "Son, do me a favor. Run down to the clubhouse and get me a candy bar. My sugar is dropping."

"I ran down there and came back," Robinson said. "After he ate that candy bar, he outdrove me by 20 yards. He was 77 years old!"

***

Retired Canton Police Detective Jim Mitchell recalled Motley always having a presence at a local downtown restaurant called the Mayfair Tavern, which was a regular lunch spot for a lot of people in Canton—judges, police officers, postal workers, like Motley was at the time, and regular folks.

"You would think he wouldn't take time to talk with guys that are not important, but he always felt, we always felt, comfortable around Marion," Mitchell said. "We talked about the Browns, things that he was doing at the time in his job with the Postal Service, and things of that nature. He didn't select who he wanted to talk with or sit with. He'd just come in there and sit down . . .

it could be a police officer, an attorney, a dentist from down the street that used to always show up with a group of dentists, or it could be just a regular guy. He'd come and sit down. He was typical like that."

Greg Walker, Motley's nephew, said: "I remember him as a monumental individual. He was a fantastic guy with a big heart. He loved humanity and expressed that in the way he lived." Walker also chauffeured his uncle around in the late 1990s. Walker said his thrill was driving Motley from Cleveland to the Hall of Fame to pick up his mail there. Walker said his uncle enjoyed listening to jazz, and he recalled one memory when he inadvertently turned Motley on to a new jazz station.

"He was a big kind of classical and jazz music fan," Walker said. "There was this new jazz station in Cleveland called 107.3 The Wave that I switched to when he was out of the car. When he got back in, we drove around for a few hours listening to that station and he said, 'You know what? That's a really good station. Don't ever touch that radio station. You leave it right where it is.'"

***

As time moved on, Motley didn't move as fast. However, he stayed true to what his grandson Joe Dose described as a "laid back" and "chill" way of life. Motley's driving, though, was another story. In the summer of 1979, he was driving his car in suburban Cleveland. He wasn't speeding, wasn't driving impaired, and wasn't driving erratically, but he hit the car in front of him. There weren't any injuries. It was a "fender-bender." Motley, who blamed an oil slick on the road for causing him to lose control of his car, was cited, and he pleaded no contest to the offense of following too close.

Shaker Heights Municipal Court Judge Frank Spiegel waived

the $10 fine. (Motley did pay $13 in court fees). "Well, I find you guilty but suspend any fine in consideration of the great pleasure you gave the community in your playing days," Judge Spiegel said.

***

For all the individual memories people have of Motley, Canton native and *Canton Repository* writer Charita Goshay said she was amazed at the number of people who live in Canton, and Northeast Ohio, who have never heard of Marion Motley, or aren't aware of him apart from a signpost on the street that was named in his honor in the neighborhood where he grew up.

"Canton is a city that had a crisis of confidence, and there's nothing like a hero from your own hometown to make you feel better about yourself," Goshay said. "Marion Motley, he was never a chest thumping kind of guy. . . . He was typical of Canton. He had charisma when he walked into the room, and when he walked in, you knew he was in the room. He lived close to the ground, he worked hard, and did what he needed to do, and made the most of his talent. That's why Canton needs to pay more attention (to him.)"

CHAPTER 22

ANOTHER MOTLEY FIRST

Making history ran in the Motley family. Or maybe it was the fact that Marion Motley's life, and the way he lived it, resonated so profoundly with his family members that it drove them to become the best at whatever they endeavored. That was the case with Motley's granddaughter, Bianca Motley Broom.

Motley Broom was the daughter of Raymond, Marion and Eula's middle son. A Cleveland native, she went on to get her undergraduate degree from Duke University, a law degree from Washington University, and then an MBA from Lake Forest Graduate School of Management. After more than a decade as a trial attorney and litigator, and then a stint as part-time judge on the Fulton County Magistrate Court, she was elected mayor of College Park, a suburb just outside of Atlanta. When sworn in as mayor in January 2020, Motley Broom became the first woman and the first Black person to hold that position.

In a 2022 interview, Motley Broom said her grandfather's experiences influenced her as she made her mark in her profession. "He's paved the way in so many ways for me and others," she said.

"I draw upon his experiences now. I think about what it was like for him to be the first, and how he paved the way for people, and how there were so many people before him who probably could have done really, really well, but didn't have the opportunity. And I think about that in terms of this role as well. How many women, how many people of color in the 125 years of this city have not had the chance to serve? And I feel like I draw upon his strength."

Bianca Motley Broom was elected mayor of College Park, Georgia, in 2019.

Motley Broom said it took years for her and other next-generation family members to realize what their grandfather accomplished on and off the field. "He told the stories about the sheer injustice that he dealt with, just trying to make a living as a professional football player, but it wasn't like those were stories that popped up during the course of conversation," she said. "I don't know that it really sank in for me as a kid, because I was born in 1977. His experience was so far removed from my own. It was sort of hard to even wrap your head around what he and the others went through.

"Football is a tough sport," she continued, "but the kind of abuse he experienced, along with Bill Willis, as well as Kenny Washington and Woody Strode, was unbelievable, especially what my grandfather and Bill experienced in the South. We kind of took it for granted."

Duke isn't a school known for its great football teams, and that held true during Motley Broom's time in Durham during the late 1990s. "Duke football was terrible when I was there." Motley Broom said.

"Yeah, the football team was bad," she continued. "We went defeated my sophomore year." In fact, the 1996 season was one of three in the span of six years when the Blue Devils went 0–11. But during her junior year, she said the skies opened. The football gods had mercy, and in the flash of a first down, a field goal, and fandemonium, the Duke Blue Devils finally won a football game.

"The students tore down the goal post and took it all across campus," she recounted proudly. All she knew was that the players and the fans were elated because of just one win—a win that was a long time coming.

Then she quickly remembered something. "When I got into Duke for my undergrad, my grandfather said, 'They sent me a letter trying to recruit me, and I wrote back and I told them, 'Are you sure you want me? Because I'm Black.' He said, 'I never heard from them again.'"

It was the same thing Motley experienced when Clemson was recruiting him. When word got back to Clemson that Motley was Black, the school was no longer interested.

That's why Motley Broom said she reflects on the way her grandfather always showed composure, poise, and self-control when she is working in her job as a mediator or engaging with the city council.

"I always try to respond by being very measured, like my grandfather," she said. "He wasn't the kind of person who would lose his temper, get angry, or overreact. He let his play on the field speak for itself. And I think that in almost every arena, I do my best to let my work speak for itself. I let the results speak. I think that's a pretty strong and direct Motley trait."

CHAPTER 23

LOSING A LEGEND

As the years passed, Jackie Robinson's name was written into sports immortality. And he earned it. During 10 seasons with the Brooklyn Dodgers, he proved to be not just a pioneer but a bona fide superstar. He was named to six All-Star Games and earned the 1949 National League MVP Award. Brooklyn won six NL pennants and the 1955 World Series with him on the roster. And wherever he went, fans came out in droves to see him—whether because of his historic nature or his electrifying base running.

Though overt racism followed Robinson throughout his playing days, today baseball universally celebrates its first Black player. His No. 42 jersey is retired across Major League Baseball, except on April 15—Jackie Robinson Day—when everyone on the field wears it. His story was even chronicled in a feature film, *42*, that was released in 2013. And all the accolades are deserved.

Those close to Marion Motley can't help but notice that he's not celebrated in the same way. Many people today don't even know that Motley—and Woody Strode, Kenny Washington, and Bill Willis—broke the color line first.

"I always said that all due respect to Jackie Robinson, nice job. (But) it happened first in pro football. It truly did," said Dave Motts, the longtime executive at the Pro Football Hall of Fame. "Pro football wasn't mainstream like baseball, but the color barrier was really broken by those gentlemen, and a coach named Paul Brown, who said if all his (Black) players couldn't do something together they didn't do it. If their Black players were not allowed (somewhere), then they weren't staying. We always found that heartening and we always kind of wore a patch because it showed that pro football really reintegrated sports."

In fact, according to former Hall of Fame Executive Director Joe Horrigan, Motley and Willis played an influential role in Robinson's breakthrough. Branch Rickey, an Ohio native, was the Dodgers' general manager who signed Robinson. Before he did, "Rickey watched Motley and Willis play with the Browns—and watched that fans were reacting positively to them," Horrigan said. "And Marion Motley once told me that he used to carry a newspaper clip in which Branch Rickey told the story that it was because of watching Marion Motley and Bill Willis play pro football, a contact sport, successfully, and the fact that fans responded well, and there were no on-the-field incidents, that gave him the courage, as he put it, to invite Jackie Robinson to play in the major leagues in 1947."

Motley echoed that story in an interview with the *Philadelphia Daily News*. "Jackie's signing got a lot more (attention) because baseball was much bigger than pro football in the '40s," Motley said. "What we did helped Jackie get into the major leagues. There was a quote from Branch Rickey who said, 'If these men can play a contact sport like football, then Jackie Robinson can play baseball.' So, we really opened the door in two sports."

Not long after Robinson broke baseball's color line with the Dodgers, the Cleveland Indians signed Larry Doby, making him the American League's first Black player and MLB's second. Before taking the field for the first time in July 1947, Doby contacted Motley and Willis to ask what it was like to be a professional athlete in Cleveland. "We always found that interesting as well as a side note of history that not only did pro football reintegrate professional sports, but it had a hand in integrating baseball, America's national pastime," Motts said.

So when people talk about Jackie Robinson as the barrier-breaking Black superstar, those close to Motley hope they'll also think about those who came before. "It's not about that singular person, because there are people that paved the way for Jackie Robinson," said Tony Motley, one of Marion's grandsons. "But the story hasn't been told or said enough that there were people that came before him."

Motley's career was recognized with his 1968 induction into the Pro Football Hall of Fame. After that, he gradually faded out of the public eye.

In the late 1990s, Motley was diagnosed with prostate cancer. On June 27, 1999, after more than a year battling the disease, he died at his son Raymond's home in Cleveland. Motley was 79 years old.

The death was notable enough to earn an obituary in the *New York Times*. "Marion Motley, Bruising Back For Storied Browns, Dies at 79," the headline read. In a story in the next edition of *Sports Illustrated*, the senior writer Paul Zimmerman lamented that "the world never saw the real Marion Motley," because he made his NFL debut in 1950 as "a 30-year-old fullback with two bad knees."

"The real Marion Motley was the 232-pound monster who burst onto the All-America Football Conference scene in 1946 and terrorized the new league," Zimmerman wrote. "That's the man who fascinated me as a youngster."

Zimmerman ended his tribute by hedging on his previous statement that Motley was the greatest football player he'd ever seen, but not by much. "Certainly he's the greatest fullback," he wrote. "Tireless, devastating, explosive. It's hard to see how you could play the game any better than he did."

To family who cared for Motley in his final days, the memories are more personal. Grandson Tony Motley would often visit and spend quality time with his father and grandfather during that time. Tony Motley said his grandfather remained strong, a trait Marion Motley possessed his entire life. "My grandfather, being who he was, didn't want to take chemo or anything like that," Tony Motley said. "He wanted to just kind of ride it out. My grandfather was a great man. When you say gentle giant, he was really the essence of a gentle, gentle giant."

As part of the NFL's 100-year anniversary celebrations, the league named Marion Motley as one of its 100 best players of all time.

POSTSCRIPT: AUTHOR'S NOTE

Being a longtime Browns fan, I knew of Marion Motley and heard his name mentioned as one of the Browns' greatest running backs. But admittedly, I didn't know his history and never quite understood the importance of his accomplishments and his career on and off the field. That changed in 1999. In my longtime job as a sportswriter for the *Akron Beacon Journal*, I was assigned to cover Motley's funeral.

It was during this assignment that I began to realize the impact this man had on the football field. I listened to his former teammates—many of them legends in their own right—celebrate his life with family members and friends. That allowed me to look at Motley's life in a different light than I had prior to covering his funeral. I think it was a blessing and a gift for me.

In that story, which ran on Friday, July 2, 1999, I wrote about the nearly 400 people who showed up at Mount Sinai Baptist Church, on the east side of Cleveland. Many of the names who figured prominently in this book were there—Hall of Famers Paul Warfield, Lou Groza, and Dante Lavelli among them. But so were others who had never met Motley.

"I never saw Mr. Motley play but as a die-hard Browns fan, I thought it was my duty to be here," one man told me. "I just had to come here and represent all of the die-hard Browns fans who couldn't be here but appreciate everything Mr. Motley did for the Browns and who he was as a person."

Several people close to Motley spoke of him that day, perhaps none more glowingly than Emerson Cole, a Browns teammate from 1950 into 1952. One of the rare Black players on the team at that time, Cole said Motley supported him even after the Browns cut him. Upon returning home, Cole found $500 in his bank account from Motley. "Pay me back whenever you can," the Hall of Famer told him.

"He should have been an ambassador," Cole said. "Motley was the leader. He kept peace between us and the larger group. He made the rules and he was big enough to enforce them. He knew a stupid act by any of us would affect many, many people that would come after us. We had to have impeccable character."

As I look back, and look forward, it was astonishing how my life crossed paths with this amazing man, Marion Motley, again in the decades to come. After covering Motley's funeral that day, I wrote about him again about a month later. That fall, the Browns were making their return to the NFL as an expansion team after a three-year absence caused by Art Modell's shady deal that sent the original Browns to Baltimore, where they became the Ravens. But in 1999, all that mattered for fans in Cleveland was that the "new" Browns were back. The *Beacon Journal* decided to run a 99-day countdown to the Browns' return—which came in the annual Hall of Fame Game in Canton against the Dallas Cowboys—and every day during the countdown, the number corresponded with a number relating to the Browns. I was assigned several numbers, one of which was No. 36, which Motley wore for part of his career. Again, another coincidental blessing for me, because after learning so much about Motley's legacy at his funeral, I was given the opportunity to learn even more while doing research for this assignment.

This article ran on Saturday, August 7, 1999. It ended with a quote from Larry Phillips, the Ohio sports historian who was quoted extensively in this book.

"He should be an icon, a civic icon, in Canton, just because of his impact at the high school level, and at the professional level," Phillips said. "To this day, Canton McKinley and the Cleveland Browns are part of the fabric of the community, and he was the star of both of those entities. I believe he is an icon among the historians of the sport."

Though my career took me in different directions after that, my interest and admiration in Motley only grew. Around 20 years later I was proud and honored to be part of the team that told Motley's story in video form as a co-producer for the documentary *Lines Broken: The Story of Marion Motley*. The film, which premiered on PBS Western Reserve in 2021, went on to win a regional Emmy in the Documentary Historical category.

Producing the film coincided with another team of colleagues, the Marion Motley Memorial Fund Committee, which raised money to have a statue made of Motley and placed near the Pro Football Hall of Fame. The money was raised—more than $100,000 from so many sources—over a five-year period. The groundbreaking ceremony took place July 30, 2021, at Stadium Park, located just east of the I-77 underpass and entrances to the Hall of Fame and Tom Benson Stadium. The city of Canton, led by Mayor Thomas M. Bernabei, and the Hall of Fame, led by then president and CEO David Baker, were amazingly cooperative.

Flash forward to August 3, 2022. That was the day of the unveiling of the 8', free-standing bronze statue of Motley's likeness. More than 200 supporters attended the event, including so many members of the Motley family from Northeast Ohio. Some traveled from as far away as Georgia and Texas for the special event. It was a quite a journey, from the inception of the idea to that day. But it was long overdue.

Two of Marion Motley's grandchildren, Joe Dose, *left*, and Bianca Motley Broom, pose in front of the Marion Motley statue at its unveiling in Canton, Ohio.

One of the highlights was seeing Las Vegas Raiders head coach Josh McDaniels take his team to the statue. The Raiders were playing in the annual Hall of Fame Game against the Jacksonville Jaguars, and it was a homecoming for McDaniels, who graduated from Canton McKinley High School and was the starting quarterback for his dad, head coach Thom McDaniels, when the Bulldogs were the 1997 *USA Today* national champions. Seeing McDaniels, Raiders quarterback Derek Carr, and the rest of the Raiders' team paying respect to the Motley statue and what it represented was quite an emotional moment.

Among those in attendance that day was another Canton sports legend. The name Renee Powell is legendary in both the golf world and in Ohio. She began golfing at the age of three at Clearview Golf Club in East Canton, the only golf course designed, built, owned, and operated by an African American: her father, William J. Powell.

Powell's significance in the sport is immense. She was captain of the women's golf team at Ohio University and then at Ohio State University, and then became just the second Black woman on the Ladies Professional Golf Association Tour. (As of 2021 only six more had joined that list.) She eventually competed in 250 professional golf tournaments and racked up a seemingly endless list of accolades, including being named the Professional Golfers Association First Lady of Golf in 2003, being inducted into the Ohio Women's Hall of Fame, becoming the first female golfer to receive an honorary doctor of laws degree from St. Andrew's University in Scotland, and being recognized nationally as a top instructor. Powell and her family also established the Clearview

Legacy Foundation for education, preservation, and research. When Powell speaks, her words carry weight, especially in Canton.

Motley's legacy has been celebrated in Canton, most notably at the Hall of Fame. Thirty-four years later, in 2002, the city renamed a street in the northeast part of town for Motley, though critics pointed out that the street is in a part of town that can hardly be considered nice. Supporters of Motley long wanted more. With the statue, they finally got a more fitting tribute. But as Powell pointed out, there can—and should—still be more.

"Marion was a person in our own community who has done so much," Powell said. "The Hall of Fame lives to recognize the legends, but this legend is not even acknowledged in the community for who he was. Why has it taken so long to build something in honor of him? Why is it that Black legends are only recognized by streets in the worst ghettos?"

MARION MOTLEY: STATS AT A GLANCE

Born: June 5, 1920, in Leesburg, Georgia
Died: June 27, 1999, in Cleveland, Ohio (age 79)

Positions: Fullback, Linebacker
Size: 6'1", 232 pounds
Pro Teams: Cleveland Browns (1946–1953)*, Pittsburgh Steelers (1955)
* *1946–49 AAFC*

Offense

			Games		Rushing					Receiving					Total
Year	Age	Tm	G	GS	Rush	Yds	TD	Lng	Avg	Rec	Yds	TD	Lng	Avg	Yds
1946	26	CLE	13	10	73	601	5	76	8.2	10	188	1	63	18.8	789
1947	27	CLE	14	12	146	889	8	50	6.1	7	73	1		10.4	962
1948+	28	CLE	14	14	157	**964**	5		6.1	13	192	2	78	14.8	1156
1949	29	CLE	11	10	113	570	8		5.0	15	191	0		12.7	761
1950*+	30	CLE	12	12	140	**810**	3	69	**5.8**	11	151	1	41	13.7	961
1951	31	CLE	11	10	61	273	1	26	4.5	10	52	0	34	5.2	325
1952	32	CLE	12	10	104	444	1	59	4.3	13	213	2	68	16.4	657
1953	33	CLE	12	0	32	161	0	34	5.0	6	47	0	23	7.8	208
1955	35	PIT	6	0	2	8	0	8	4.0			0			8
Total			105	78	828	4720	31	76	5.7	85	1107	7	78	10.5	5827

Defense and Special Teams

			Games		Defense			Special Teams / Kick Returns				
Year	Age	Tm	G	GS	Int	Yds	TD	Ret	Yds	TD	Lng	Avg
1946	26	CLE	13	10	1	0	0	3	53	0		17.7
1947	27	CLE	14	12	1	48	1	13	322	0		24.8
1948+	28	CLE	14	14				14	337	0		24.1
1949	29	CLE	11	10				12	262	0		21.8
1950*+	30	CLE	12	12								
1951	31	CLE	11	10								
1952	32	CLE	12	10				3	88	0	35	29.3
1953	33	CLE	12	0				3	60	0	22	20.0
1955	35	PIT	6	0								
Total			105	78	2	48	1	48	1122	0	35	23.4

Source: Pro Football Reference

Key

+ First-Team All-Pro
* Pro Bowl
League Leader

LINES BROKEN: THE STORY OF MARION MOTLEY

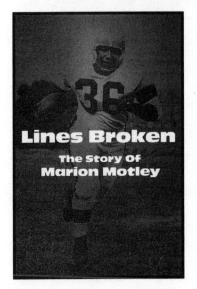

Much of the reporting in this book originated during the reporting for *Lines Broken: The Story of Marion Motley*, a half-hour documentary produced in 2021 by PBS Western Reserve and distributed nationally by American Public Television.

The documentary, for which this book's author David Lee Morgan Jr. served as a co-producer, has gone on to win several awards including a regional Emmy award in the Documentary Historical category at the 53rd Central Great Lakes Regional Emmy Awards.

The film is available for free on-demand viewing at PBSWesternReserve.org.

> **Lines Broken** tells Motley's story of adversity, personal tragedy, and triumphs using rarely heard archival interviews and new interviews with historians, friends, and descendants.

of professional football. But neither Motley's feats on the field nor his deep connection to Northeast Ohio could keep him from facing racism, a history that Morgan shares in fascinating detail."

—*David Whitehill, President and CEO of ArtsinStark and the Cultural Center for the Arts*

"This book drives home the journey Marion Motley took to reach the pinnacle of his sport. We hear so much about Jim Brown, and rightly so, but clearly Motley paved the way and was among the elite in the game in his own right. What David Lee Morgan lays out so beautifully is the story behind the success Motley fought to achieve on the field along with memorable personal stories such as how Motley and Paul Brown first met. Every sports fan should find the time to read this story for a whole new appreciation of what it means to be a champion on and off the field. Clearly Motley was both."

—*Eric Mansfield, playwright, former Cleveland journalist*

"David Lee Morgan Jr.'s book should be required reading for NFL rookies, Cleveland Browns fans, and anyone who is interested in the early history of professional football. Morgan takes the reader from the days of Marion Motley's eye-popping performances at the high school and college levels to a professional career so stellar that those who were there still recall it with reverence. The racism Motley faced throughout his life still, sadly, resonates today. Morgan pulls us into Motley's world, and we are grateful for it."

—*Jessica Whitehill, award-winning sports journalist*

"Thank you, David, for the wonderful way you told our grandfather's story. David Lee Morgan Jr.'s book is truly a tribute to Marion Motley and his legacy. It is tremendous how he interwove his career statistics, time outside of football, societal impacts, and historical events all in a straightforward narrative. It embodied the full story of his life. His accomplishments and impacts on the game of football and civil rights deserve to be known, and this book has helped further that."

—*Joe Dose, grandson of Marion Motley*

ACKNOWLEDGEMENTS

To my wife, Jill; our kids Trey, Joey, Christian, Lunden, Brooke, Jonah, and Cameron; our married-into-the-family moms, Marya and Lydia; our grandkids, Avery, Amira, and Josephine; and our four-legged kids D. J. and Donut: thank you for all the love and support.

And thank you to:
Marion Motley for his life and legacy
The Motley Family
The Pro Football Hall of Fame
The City of Canton
Hall of Famers Paul Warfield and Dave Robinson
James Waters and Joy Waters
Eric Loughry and Rachel Harris
Shaun Horrigan
Joe Horrigan
David and Jessica Whitehill
Dave Jingo
R. J. Van Almen
Antonio Hall
Jill Thomas
James Wells